GOD, GOLD, AND CIVIL GOVERNMENT

Tom Rose

American Enterprise Publications
Mercer, PA 16137-3827

American Enterprise Publications
177 N. Spring Road
Mercer, Pennsylvania 16137
724-748-3726
www.biblicaleconomics.com

Copyright ©2002 by Tom Rose
All rights reserved.

Scripture taken from the King James version.

ISBN 0-9720016-0-3
Library of Congress Control No. 2002091437

Cover design by Wayne Rongaus, Rongaus Design

Printed in the United States of America

My deepest thanks to Ruth, my wife and partner in life,
for her dedicated work as editor and helpful critic
in publishing this work.

CONTENTS

PREFACE

This book deals with the topic of Liberty. Specifically, it deals with the question of how man is to live—economically, politically, and spiritually—as a free and self-responsible individual in a world which is becoming more and more tyrannical.

All during the 20th Century Americans, and the peoples of other nations too, have lived in an age in which the institution of civil government has steadily encroached in the once-private spheres of family, church, business, and education. Today, in the early part of the 21st Century, we find individual initiative and self-responsibility of the individual consistently stymied and frustrated by a thousand-and-one governmental interventions in every aspect of our lives.

This book shows how we arrived at such a sad state, and it also enlightens the reader about how to go about reconstructing our social/political/economic order so that man can once again stand before his Creator as a precious and independent self-responsible being. ("Let my people go, that they may serve me!" Ex. 8:1.)

Liberty is like a three-legged stool. It has three aspects, or legs: the Spiritual, the Economic, and the Political. Each leg must be carefully preserved. If one leg is shortened or cut off, the stability provided by the other two will be hampered or lost, and the ideal of Liberty will come tumbling down.

This, then, presents the universal problem of—not only Americans, whose civil rulers have become tyrannical—but also the problem that faces freedom-minded people all over the world.

For whom, then, is this book written? A Chinese proverb goes something like this: "If you are building for a year, plant rice; if you are building for generations, plant acorns that will grow to be sturdy oaks." Our need today is to instill a zealous love of Liberty in all of its aspects (Spiritual, Economic, and Political) in the hearts and minds of each new generation—which is something that is *not* happening in the educational institutions that the large majority of young people are enrolled in today. Thus, my answer is that this book is written for "young hearts and minds" from the age of junior high through late adult. It should be especially useful for parents, teachers, pastors, grandparents, and anyone who is concerned about our lost liberties and how to restore them, both in our Republic and in other nations.

Some of the principles and issues dealt with are simple and straightforward; others are a bit more complex and challenging; but each is carefully and thoughtfully presented so as to be easily grasped and understood. My heartfelt wish and desire is that each reader will find this text to be a rich resource for understanding the spiritual/ economic/political scenario that faces us today, and that he or she will find enlightenment of how to live this life—and the one thereafter—as a free and self-responsible person.

Tom Rose

I
Basic Economics

1

BIBLICAL ECONOMICS: ITS SPIRITUAL ECONOMIC AND POLITICAL ASPECTS

And God said, Let us make man in our image,
after our likeness: . . .
- Genesis 1:26

I t is obvious to anyone with an understanding of the lessons of history that freedom is in decline in America. It has been for a number of generations. The question is why? The answer is that too many of our nation's moral and philosophical leaders have lost touch with the biblical foundations upon which our whole system of American culture is based (Ps.11:3).

The Importance of Biblical Presuppositions

The presuppositions one holds are important. They condition a person's world-and-life view. They predetermine whether a person will view God's created world from a humanistic or a biblical viewpoint. The presupposition of this essay is:

- The God of the Bible exists.
- It is He who created the universe and who sustains it moment by moment (Job 38:4-41).
- God directs everything according to His predetermined end (Isa. 40:21-31).

Therefore, when we consider anything about man or the world in which he lives, we must necessarily start with God.

Neutrality about God is impossible. Any person who thinks he can be neutral about God starts his thinking from an erroneous presupposition. Any attempt to be neutral about God is simply a fruitless effort to be anti-theistic. Cornelius Van Til points out in his *Survey of Christian Epistemology* that Adam and Eve were true theists before the fall because they accepted God's interpretation of themselves. But, when the tempter came along and seduced Eve into questioning God, she could listen to the tempter only by first giving up the presupposition of God's ultimacy and replacing it with an equal ultimacy between God and the devil, and herself.[1]

A Look at Man

Let us ask some fundamental questions: What is man? What is his relationship to God? What is his relationship to himself, to other men, to Satan, to the state, and to the world?

The Bible tells us that man is a created being. He didn't just "happen" to evolve by chance from a lower form of life. In Genesis we find God speaking, "Let us make man in our image, after our likeness" (Gen.1:26). What does it mean for man to be made in the image and likeness of God? What significance does it have with respect to man's spiritual, economic, and political freedom?

The fact that man is created in the very image and likeness of God is what gives man freedom and self-responsibility before God. God, by His very nature, has the ability to think rationally and to place value on things. That is, He has the power to think economically. He is the first economist. And because man is created after God's own image, man can also think and act economically. Man's ability to impute (place) value on things and to choose, that is, to act as an economic being is but a reflection of God. Man is responsible to God because he bears God's image. This, in essence, is man's spiritual/economic tie to God as his Creator. Except for the fact that man is created in God's very image, man would have no spiritual freedom (Adam had the freedom to sin or not to sin), nor would there be any science called economics. And except for this fact, neither would there be such a thing as political freedom. If man were not created in God's image and likeness, he would be nothing more than a chattel—a non-responsible being. In short, every facet of man's freedom and responsibility before God rests on the fact that he bears the sacred image of God in his soul. It is this sacred relationship between man and God that civil rulers have a duty to protect. The *only* God-given duty of civil government is to protect and to preserve the right and freedom of individuals to freely act in conformance with God's moral law.

What, then, according to God's plan, is man's relationship to God and to God's creation? In Genesis 1:27 we find that the Godhead did indeed create man as proposed in Genesis 1:26. And in 1:28 we discover man's economic role relative to God's creation:

> . . . Be fruitful, and multiply, and replenish the earth, and subdue it: and have dominion over the fish of the sea, and over the fowl of the air, and over every living thing that moveth upon the earth (Gen. 1:28).

Here we see that man is made to be an economic steward who is responsible to God for his dominion over God's gifts to him. Christian men and women (and not civil governments) are God's "spiritual house, an holy priesthood, to offer up spiritual sacrifices, acceptable to God by Jesus Christ" (I Pet. 2:5).

As a prophet, the Christian man intermediates from God toward the world in all that he thinks, says, and does. As a priest, he represents the world toward God; he dedicates the world, his work in it, and all that is in it to service to God. In short, man is to keep the world under dominion for the glory of God. In Exodus 19:6 God admonishes, "And ye shall be unto me a kingdom of priests, and an holy nation. . . ." Even the last book of the Bible stresses believing man's God-given role as priest and king. In Revelation 1:5-6 believers in heaven sing Christ's praises thus: ". . . Unto him that loved us, and washed us from our sins in his own blood, And hath made us kings and priests unto God and his Father; . . ."

Man's duty to God, which includes man's economic role as well as his spiritual role, is found in these commands:

> And now, Israel, what doth the Lord thy God require of thee, but to fear the Lord thy God, to walk in all his ways, and to love him, and to serve the Lord thy God with all thy heart and with all thy soul (Deut. 10:12).

> . . . Fear God, and keep his commandments: for this is the whole duty of man (Eccl. 12:13).

> He hath shewed thee, O man, what is good; and what doth the Lord require of thee, but to do justly, and to love mercy, and to walk humbly with thy God? (Mic. 6:8)

Mark 12:29-31 succinctly combines man's duty to both God and his fellowmen:

> . . . The first of all the commandments is, Hear, O Israel; The Lord our God is one Lord:
> And thou shalt love the Lord thy God with all thy heart, and with all thy soul, and with all thy mind, and with all thy strength: this is the first commandment.
> And the second is like, namely this, Thou shalt love thy neighbor as thyself. There is none other commandment greater than these.

Man's Relationship to Satan

There is a good reason why God admonishes man to love Him "with all thy heart, and with all thy soul, and with all thy mind, and with all thy strength." This reason comes to light when we consider man's relationship to Satan. In John 8:34 and 36 our Lord admonishes us, ". . . Whosoever committeth sin is the servant of sin. . . ." and "If the Son therefore shall make you free, ye shall be free indeed."

Even though man was created as a free and self-responsible agent, man by his very nature tends to align himself with a higher power. Though free, man is *not* a primary entity or prime mover like God is. Man by nature will align himself either with God or with Satan. Since Adam chose to align himself with Satan, man became the servant of sin and lost the spiritual freedom that God gave him at creation. Ever since Adam's fall, sinful men have been faced with the moral choice of whom they will serve, Satan or God. Joshua challenged the Old Testament Israelites with these words:

> Now therefore fear the Lord, and serve him in sincerity and truth: . . .
> . . . choose you this day whom ye will serve; . . . but as for me and my house, we will serve the Lord (Josh. 24:14-15).

Since man's political and economic freedoms are but functions, or outgrowths of his more basic spiritual freedom, it is crucially important for man to preserve his allegiance to God. In short, man by his very nature *will* choose to serve a higher power. The only question is: Will he serve Satan and thereby become a slave to sin? Or will he serve God and thus be free in accordance to God's higher law? The apostle Paul writes to regenerated men,

> For, brethren, ye have been called unto liberty; only use not liberty for an occasion to the flesh, but by love serve one another.
> For all the law is fulfilled in one word, even in this; Thou shalt love thy neighbor as thyself (Gal. 5:13-14).

Why Should Man Be Free?

A question now arises: Why should man be free? The answer to this question is very important because, unless we understand the real reason for man's God-given freedom, we aren't likely to defend invasions of our freedom by civil authorities, which is the usual source of the loss of freedom. The reason that man *should* be free, the reason that man *must guard and defend* his God-given freedom, is found in Exodus 8:1. Here we find Moses confronting Pharaoh on behalf of the Israelites who have been enslaved by the ruler of Egypt. He delivers God's ultimatum, "Let my people go!" But is that *all* God told Moses to tell Pharaoh? The answer is, "No!" The full text of Moses' ultimatum is this: "Let my people go, *that they may serve me!*" Note that the *purpose* of man's freedom is that he be free to serve God!

God's designed plan in this sinful world is for man to live as a free being, not simply for the sake of freedom in and of itself (which would be nothing more than license to do as we please), but so that *man can be free to serve God!* God *requires* that man *preserve* his freedom so that he can be *self-responsible to God* as his Creator and Sustainer. Freedom is not something for man to enjoy only if the civil rulers graciously condescend in granting him freedom. Certainly not! Freedom is *absolutely necessary* if man is to be fully self-responsible before his Creator.

Freedom is a gift *from God*, not a gift from civil rulers to be granted at their whim. For example, for me to attack or undermine another person's freedom would be to rob him of his most precious essence as a human being, his need to be self-responsible to God. The same holds true for you or the civil government, which is so often in our day the pernicious vehicle of man's enslavement. The founding fathers of America understood this truth, but too many modern Americans, including our political leaders, have either forgotten or never understood the underlying theology of economic and political freedom. Man *must* be free in order to serve God in love and in truth.

Let us never forget this: Freedom and self-responsibility are two sides of the same precious coin. One cannot exist without the other. If one is curtailed or expunged, the other will vanish in response. This is not to say, of course, that man cannot be spiritually free, even if he is imprisoned. I have become friends with a man who is now in prison, where he came to know Christ as Saviour. This man, though imprisoned, is spiritually free. But the full blossoming of his spiritual freedom into the related outer spheres of political and economic freedom await his pending release.

The Role of the State

Now we come to the very practical matter of man's relation to the civil government. This matter can best be presented by asking this question: What is the proper role of civil government in a society of God-created, free, and self-responsible individuals?

James H. Thornwell (1812-1862) pointed out that civil government is a moral agency established by God.

> . . . Civil government is an institute of Heaven, founded in the character of man as social and moral, and is designed to realize the idea of justice. . . . As the State is essentially moral in its idea, it connects itself directly with the government of God. . . . A State, therefore, which does not recognize its dependence upon God, or which fails to apprehend, in its functions and offices, a commission from heaven, is false to the law of its own being. . . .[2]

It is in I Timothy 2 that we find a biblical statement of the proper role of civil government and its relationship to man. In this passage Paul tells us to pray for all men, and especially "for kings and for all that are in authority." Then he goes on to explain *why* we should pray for civil rulers. We are admonished to pray for them "that we may lead a quiet and peaceable life in all godliness and honesty" (I Tim. 2:1-2).

Paul's explanation is of great importance because it instructs us regarding God's objective in establishing the institution of civil government and its proper role in a free society where men are self-responsible to God during their temporary sojourn on earth. The only proper biblical role of civil government is to maintain a moral system of law and order so that man can be free and responsible before God. Civil government is a God-instituted social agency, not to restrict man's freedom, but to *maximize* man's personal freedom and self-responsibility to his Creator.

Thornwell recognized this truth because, in the quote above, he went on to state that, "Subjects that have no religion are incapable of law. . . ."[3] If man were an evolved being, as the humanistic Darwinian evolutionists suppose him to be, man would not stand as a self-responsible being before God; nor would there be a need for a social agency called civil government to preserve and enhance man's freedom. In matter of fact, the humanistic evolutionary view of man leads naturally to totalitarian forms of civil government which enslave men and turn them into chattel. (Another whole essay can be written on this.)

As it is, because of man's fallen nature, and because of his sinful tendency to enslave and take unfair advantage of his fellowmen, the institution of civil government is God's appointed means of *preserving* and *maximizing* man's freedom and responsibility before God. There is a saying that goes like this: "That which is not free cannot be self-responsible." Thus, the spread of freedom, and not the encroachment of people's freedom, is the only valid end of civil government.

Today, we find civil rulers all over the world busily arrogating to themselves, contrary to God's moral law, the responsibility of maintaining full employment, of stimulating the economy, of "protecting" the people from their own supposed shortsightedness, of eliminating poverty, and of using the state's taxing power to forcibly transfer wealth from some citizens to others. In short, modern-day humanistic rulers use the guise of caring for the people "from the cradle to the grave" as a means of plundering the people to further their own political and economic goals. This is the mark of modern totalitarianism, the mark of the beast spoken of in the book of Revelation. Today we see it growing by leaps and bounds here in America; and we also see it in every nation of the world. It is the result of man's widespread religious apostasy and the general flight from biblical precepts. It turns God's institution of civil government from a moral agency designed to protect and maximize man's freedom and self-responsibility before God into an immoral humanistic agency of outright political and economic tyranny.

As Christians who stand free and responsible before God for our actions and for the wealth we control while sojourning on this earth, we should be aware of the widespread tendency of civil rulers to depart from their God-appointed role. And we should set about to reform and to reconstruct our social institutions, especially that of civil government. Our goal in doing this is to maximize each person's individual freedom and self-responsibility before God. (The questions of man's sinfulness, of man's control of property, and of the role of voluntary exchange in a society of free individuals are also pertinent to the issue under discussion, but limited space requires that these be treated elsewhere.)

Notes:

1 Cornelius Van Til, A Survey of Christian Epistemology, In Defense of Biblical Christianity Series, (n.p., den Dulk Christian Foundation, 1969), 20-22.
2 The Collected Writings of James Henry Thornwell, ed. John B. Adger and John L. Girardeau, vol. 4, Ecclesiastical ([Guildford and London: The Banner of Truth Trust, 1875; reprint, 1974]), 514-515 (page references are to reprint edition).
3 Ibid., 515.

2

AN EXPRESSLY BIBLICAL
APPROACH TO ECONOMICS

. . . Thus saith the Lord, Let my people go, that
they may serve me.

- Exodus 8:1

Years ago, when I was still a religious agnostic, I was opposed to Christianity because most of the Christians with whom
I was acquainted adhered to a socialist/statist ideology. Some
of the strongest expounders of this left-leaning statism were
pastors of Christian churches.

"If this is what the Bible teaches," I reasoned, "then I don't
want anything to do with it!"

But, unknown to me at that time, the Holy Spirit was indeed working in my life. A business associate where I worked
was a "Bible thumper." He was always coming into my office to
"needle" me about the Bible. One day he advised me that the
various theological books I was reading in my search for an
unchanging and everlasting righteousness were just leading me
further and further away from Christ. Then he asked, "Tom,
how much of the Bible have you read?" My friend's name was
Seldon Brown, and we worked for the Associated Industries of
Missouri in St. Louis.

I replied, "I guess I haven't been fair about this, have I?"
So I went out at lunch time and bought a King James Bible at a
downtown "5 and 10" store.

When my friend passed by my office after lunch and looked in, I waved the Bible at him, and he said, "I know exactly what you're going to do. You're going to read that Bible with the intent of disproving every word in it, aren't you?"

"Of course," I replied.

"You can't read it that way! You have to read it prayerfully," he replied.

"How can I read it prayerfully, Seldon? I don't even know if there is a God to pray to!"

But, instead of getting a rise out of him, as I expected, Seldon just looked me in the eye and sternly retorted, "That's *your* problem!" Then he spun on his heel and walked out!

That night I took the Bible, got down on my knees and said a prayer that was honest, though a bit different from the prayers I now pray: "Oh God, if there is a God, and if this is your word, speak to me through it."

God answered that prayer, and thus began a spiritual and intellectual journey of enquiry which was destined to change, not only my world-and-life view, but also my career.

I started reading at Genesis 1:1. And as I read, it became overwhelmingly clear that the collectivist ideology that so many of the Christians whom I encountered were espousing evidently did *not* come from the Bible! For I discovered that the Bible expounds, explicitly and consistently, a position that upholds man's individual freedom and self-responsibility before God. Accordingly, the Bible did not, as I had erroneously believed, come anywhere near to endorsing the centralization of power in the hands of civil authorities, but rather just the opposite. Nor did the Bible look with favor on monetary inflation to "stimulate" the economy, nor manipulation of the economy through fiscal or monetary policies. Nor did it approve of government "transfer payments" to help the poor, to subsidize or assist other "needy" groups, business firms, or occupations. All such government interventions and so-called "transfer payments" are nothing more than forms of "legalized theft." But I did find the Bible to be consistently adamant about the moral principles "Thou shalt not steal" and "Thou shalt not covet," which apply equally to individuals and organizations as well as to civil rulers.

My discovery in the Bible of the unchanging and everlasting righteousness, which I had hungered after for so long, worked to lower my mental resistance to the truth of the Bible. God's word changed my hardened mind-set, the Holy Spirit wooed my heart, and in short order I joyously discovered that I had been one of God's elect from before the foundation of the world.

What follows is an expressly biblical approach to economics. It has been gradually developed over the years by constantly searching Scripture and then attempting to apply God's thoughts (II Cor.10:3-5) to the science of economics, which might be better defined as "man's work in God's world."

The Importance of Assumptions

Some years ago I was invited to serve on a debate panel with two other economists. One was to speak on the biblical basis of socialism. Another was to speak on the biblical basis of, believe it or not, Keynesianism. And I was to speak on the biblical basis of the free market. In my introductory remarks, I warned the audience that each of us would be presenting ideas that conflicted and that each of us would claim the Bible supported the position that each speaker expounded. But I pointed out that the Bible could not support such diametrically opposed views; that some of us, no doubt, would be expressing *Satanic* ideas, and that it was up to the audience to evaluate and weigh what each of us had to say with reference to biblical precepts.

How is it that three economists, each claiming to be a Christian, could look to the Bible for support of such opposing "brands" of economics? Is it that *any* system of economics can legitimately be defined as harmonious with biblical precepts, and that the real issue depends upon the economist's presuppositions? (As economists, we were all aware of the warning: "Don't accept an economist's model without first checking out his assumptions!") I remember being interviewed to teach economics at a Christian college that wanted a professor who would teach from a biblical basis. The interview went well until I discovered that the college administration wanted the professor they would hire to take an agnostic position on the question of ideology. In short, the administration felt that, from an economic standpoint, socialism (which includes fascism) and the competitive free market were both equally acceptable. When I insisted that the free-market system of economics is the *only* one that is compatible with Scripture, our mutual interest quickly ended.

Or, perhaps, is the real truth concerning economics that the Bible has nothing at all to do with the so-called "science" of economics, since the study of economics is purely a matter, as some economists claim, of searching for cause-effect patterns through the positivistic process of applying the scientific method?[1]

For example, I once attended an economics seminar in Chicago. During a coffee break, one of the speakers overheard some attendees discussing a "normative"[2] economic issue. At the next session the speaker digressed a few minutes to make this assertion:

> "Look," he said, "I'm a professional economist. As such, I don't get involved in choosing or weighing the moral or ethical aspects of the projects I'm hired for. If I did so, I would immediately lose my status as a professional. Thus, it's up to my employers—a business corporation, foundation, or government—to choose the ends they desire. As a professional economist, my only job is to show those who hire me the most efficient means of achieving the ends they have already chosen!"

After his talk, I approached that positive practitioner of economic science and engaged him in conversation. After verifying that he *really* meant to say what he did, I asked, "But haven't you just accurately described the viewpoint of a professional prostitute when she sells her services?" He, of course, was highly offended that a fellow-economist would suggest that his line of operation resulted in his prostituting his services.

This true story helps us focus on just one of the problems that practitioners of so-called "positive" economics must deal with, that is, the false dichotomy that modern science attempts to establish between man-the-economist and man-the-moralist. It simply cannot be done if one has any degree of moral integrity!

Lastly, when considering the Bible and economics, is it possible that the Bible perhaps *does* have something to say about economics, but *only* in the 'normative' aspect of economics in which the economist is confronted with evaluating choices that directly impinge on moral issues? I have often advised my students that "man-the-moralist must always look over the shoulder of man-the-economist, to make sure that he is headed in the right direction!"

In order to adequately answer the question "What is an expressly biblical approach to economics?," we must start with fundamentals. First, we must remind ourselves *what* the study of economics deals with: It deals with man. It deals with how man acts economically in the world that God created. Second, we must define it. I define *economics* as the science of choice: The science, or study, of how man values alternative choices, and how he acts in implementing those choices in order to maximize his sense of well-being. You will note that this definition is somewhat broader than the dictionary definition of economics, that economics is "a social science concerned chiefly with description and analysis of production, distribution and consumption of goods and services." Such a definition of economics is practically worthless because it does not focus on the individual, who is the center of all economic thinking and activity.

Since the real study of economics deals with man and how he chooses, we should take yet a third step in order to answer the question, "What is biblical economics?" That is, we should see what the Bible has to say about man—his origin, his role in life, as well as his destiny. In short, we must always remember that God is the author and controller of all law, including economic law, and that man's role is to discover and to apply God's law in God's created universe!

Now, at this point, fairness requires that I should make some of my implicit assumptions explicit for all to see: I accept the Bible as the God-breathed word of God, and that it speaks authoritatively to *every aspect of man's life,* including the study of economics (II Tim. 3:16-17). Furthermore, I operate from a presupposition that the Bible has worthwhile light to shed, not only on the aspects of *normative* economics, but also on the *positive* aspects as well.

In answer to the question of whether or not there is such a thing as "Christian" economics, my answer is both **yes** and **no**. It is *no* in the sense that a Christian economist will use many of the theorems,[3] theories,[4] and economic models that his secular counterparts customarily use. My own leaning on this question, perhaps, can best be discerned by the titles of two texts I have written on economics. They both are entitled: Economics: . . . from a Christian *perspective*[5] rather than "Christian economics." Let's take a couple of ordinary-life examples: Before my wife, Ruth, and I accepted Christ as our personal Saviour, she used to bake biscuits for breakfast two or three times a week. After we were saved, she continued the same practice, but she didn't change her biscuit recipe. Thus, her salvation didn't affect her practice of baking one iota. Of course, there were other areas of our household management that *did* change after we became Christians, especially those dealing with value orientation. But over the years, as we became more health-conscious, we discovered that the modern food chain, which emphasizes highly processed foods, was detrimental to consumers' health. As we searched more intensively for more healthful natural foods, we became ever-more appreciative of the biblical admonition to preserve our bodies as the "temple of God" (I Cor. 3:16 & 17)[6].

Take another example: Mr. Brown is the manager of the produce department in a supermarket. His customers sometimes complain that his packaged fruit and vegetables often contain spoiled items. Mr. Brown now comes to know the Lord. After this heart-changing encounter, is it unreasonable to expect Mr. Brown to show more care in packaging his fruit and vegetables? Good business practice alone would suggest such improved care after customer complaints, but the leading of the Holy Spirit would practically insure it. This is a good example of how the application of biblical theology, through changed hearts, leads to good economics and honorable business practices.

The point I am making in these examples is that a person's theology should beneficially affect the practice of economics in every aspect of life: personally at home, in one's career, and in one's relationship with others.

My "yes" answer to whether or not there is such a thing as "Christian" economics goes something like this: Christian economics is simply the application of biblical precepts[7] and insights[8] to the study of economics. Having said this, let's recognize that the Bible can be applied or misapplied in many different ways, depending upon one's *a priori*[9] and one's relative state of Christian maturity, which is always changing—hopefully, in the direction of bringing all thought captive to the mind of Christ. In spite of this potential "*a priori* hazard" and maturity problem, it is my belief that one *can* confidently rely on the Bible to shed meaningful light and give meaningful direction in the study of economics, both in the so-called "positive" and "normative" spheres into which the study has been artificially divided.

Taking Bible in Hand . . .

Let us, then, take Bible in hand and investigate in a practical way how God's word can indeed shed needed light on man, on man's purpose in life, and on man's economic activity while he temporarily sojourns in God's created world. Though there are many potential applications, we will select only a relatively few:

Genesis 1:26-27: Man is made in the very image and likeness of God. Man, therefore, is free and has a *right to be free* because he is God's image bearer. Also, for the same reason, man is an *economic being*. That is, he is able to think, to impute value, and to mentally rank his imputed values on a comparative scale so that he can make intelligent choices. Man engages in the mental process in the very same way that God does. If man were not created in the very image and likeness of God, he would be incapable of making mental value imputations,[10] and there would, therefore, be no such thing as the study of economics.

This observation, by the way, is a *positive* application of the Bible to the study of economics. Note, too, that God's dominion mandate to man was made in relation to man's covenantal role as head of the family. This, as well as other verses, brings us face to face with the biblical concept of *sphere law*,[11] which serves to *decentralize* social power structures into the separate spheres of self, family, church, voluntary organizations (like schools, business firms, clubs, etc.), and civil government. This Genesis passage, and others, therefore suggest a *decentralized* economic system which emphasizes man's right to *individual* freedom and self-responsibility before God.

Genesis 1:27-28: Man stands in direct covenantal relationship to God with respect to his role as vice-regent over God's creation. In order to exert dominion over God's creation, man must be *free* to do so. Without economic freedom to act, man cannot properly be held fully responsible by God for his actions. Thus, God's cultural mandate to man also calls for *maximum economic freedom* coupled with *maximal responsibility* to God. Maximal responsibility of self to God can best be achieved in a society in which voluntarism is practiced. This is nothing more than a functioning "free market" system, which is defined as the voluntary exchange of goods and services between free and self-responsible individuals before God.

Genesis 3:1-19: Man sinned! Therefore, the natural economic scarcity (a result of man's being created as a finite being) that existed even before man's fall was exacerbated in intensity. Thus, man is condemned in this fallen world to continual economic struggle simply to survive. Civil rulers who attempt to build Utopias here on earth through economic intervention might well take this passage to heart; for rulers are not only finite beings with limitations to their knowledge and ability, but they are sin-burdened just as much, if not more so, than the citizens over whom they exert hegemony. As a result of both their created finiteness and sin burden, civil rulers cannot be trusted with the heady experience of centralized political or economic power. They are always certain to abuse it! The Kentucky Resolution, passed by the Kentucky State House of Representatives on November 10, 1798, and concurred unanimously by the Kentucky State Senate three days later, recognized the sinful tendency of civil rulers to impose tyranny:

> In questions of power then let no more be heard of confidence in man, but bind him down from mischief by the chains of the Constitution.[12]

Jeremiah 17:5, 7, 9, 10: Man's heart is deceitful and desperately wicked. Therefore, as we have already indicated, it is not safe to allow fallen men to rule over others. The dilemma is that *all* men are sinful and cannot be trusted. So what is the solution? The answer is *a strictly limited civil authority* which serves to repress the natural outworking of man's evil heart in society so that voluntary exchange will be maximized and the use of coercive force minimized. The very existence of evil in the world *requires* some institutional arrangement to deter the outworking of evil from man's heart and which will foster the reign of voluntarism. For instance, it would be a breach of an important biblical principle for me, or you, or the civil authority, or even the elders of a church, to dictate to someone else how he should spend his income or direct his tithe to God. To do so would be a pompous and blatant act of tyranny because the control of another man's abilities, income, and wealth is solely his *own* responsibility before God. God reserves to himself sole authority for searching the heart and trying the reins of men's hearts. It is not a responsibility that can legitimately or safely be entrusted to any other earthly entity. Yet, how often do we see individuals, civil rulers, and sometimes even church leaders judging the spending and giving of others? It is this mind-set and practice that fuels the growth of centralized civil government and the so-called "welfare state" which we have observed for most of the last 100 years in our American Republic.

A few more words should be directed, at this point, to man's inner sin problem and God's outward provision for man's living in a sinful world without tyranny and utter chaos being the result. Consider this: Yes, it is true that man's heart always turns toward evil, and that he cannot therefore be trusted in positions of authority (Gen. 6:5). Yet God *has* made a unique provision to stem the outward working of man's evil heart. He has done so through a combination of man's very God-given nature in conjunction with the proper functioning of civil government, the only valid *coercive* social institution, which God himself instituted.

How does this God-instituted synergistic combination of sinful man and coercive civil government function? It works like this, and it depends upon a great big "IF." *IF* the civil authority faithfully performs its God-given role of maintaining lawful peace and order (I Tim. 2:1-2; Rom.13:1-7), then *outward* social harmony results, in spite of man's *inward* evil heart. As long as civil rulers faithfully fulfill their God-given responsibility to punish evil-doers, then no person or entity in society will be able to tyrannize anyone else by wrongly imposing his will on another. The beneficial result of this proper functioning of the civil authority is that all men will then be forced by law to enhance their own well-being *only* through the peaceful process of *voluntary* exchange. And, each person, because he is self-interested, will agree to engage in economic exchanges in a free market scenario *only* if he perceives that he will be better off after an exchange than before the exchange takes place.

What does this mean in practice? It means that neither person in a potential exchange will proceed to finalize the exchange unless the perceived benefit of what he receives is *greater* in value than what he surrenders in the exchange. This guarantees that *both* parties to a voluntary exchange will benefit. How can this be so? Because each party to the exchange process mentally imputes a *higher* value on what he receives than on what he gives in payment. If this were not so, then one or the other would abort the exchange process. Forced exchanges always benefit one party at the expense of another. Only voluntary exchange guarantees that *both* participating parties are better off after the exchange than before.

If civil rulers are truly interested in the economic welfare of the citizens over whom they bear rule (and is there any office holder who would deny that he does?), then they would be very careful to apply God's higher law evenly and without bias. Thus, voluntarism would abound, and unlawful force to tyrannize others would be quickly punished. In such a peaceful atmosphere, the general economic and social welfare of mankind would be fostered; and man's right and duty to stand self-responsible before God likewise would be maximized.

Genesis 10:8-10, 11:1-9: God's response, to Nimrod's attempt at building history's first worldwide totalitarian state at Babel, was to confuse the language, scatter the people, and divide the lands. Thus we see that God's plan for man in a sinful world is to move toward a decentralization of power and towards a one-to-one basis for economic exchange. This is a movement towards free-market exchange rather than towards a system of centralized economic control and government-directed exchange, which is exactly what we see occurring in the world today. The centralization of power leads inescapably to tyranny and to the subsequent loss of man's freedom and self-responsibility before God. This point is especially important for Christian patriots to be aware of and concerned about. Why? Because there are hidden forces in our own country and in other countries of the world who are in the late stages of quietly dismantling our constitutional republic with the objective of melding it into a one-world, fascistic state under the United Nations.

Exodus 8:1: Man has not only the right to be free, but he has the *duty* to preserve his freedom. Why is this so? Because in no other way can man be held accountable to God for his actions. Note that the purpose of freedom is not freedom simply for the sake of being fully free (which would be nothing more than a license to sin), but rather freedom for the purpose of serving God (Eccl.12:13-14). Likewise, economic freedom isn't simply for the sake of enjoying unfettered license without any moral restraints; rather, its purpose is to allow mankind maximum freedom in enlisting all of his resources—his personal gifts, and his physical wealth and financial resources—in the challenging service of faithfully building the Kingdom of God until Christ returns. This is really what Christian reconstruction is all about.

Once I gave a lecture at a faculty forum at a Christian college. I spoke on the voluntary exchange of goods and services (the free-market process) and how it is the *only* system of economic exchange that squares with biblical precepts. A professor in the History department took strong exception. He held to the idea that man, in his God-given freedom, had the free choice of opting for either a free-market system or one of the non-free systems like socialism, fascism, or communism.

I explained that God does *not* give man freedom, only to give it up in exchange for some form of totalitarian "ism" because, in doing so, he would pervert God's mandate that man is responsible for self to God. Totalitarian systems rob man of his *duty* to be responsible for all of his actions to God.

Exodus 31:1-5: This passage informs us that God gave Bezaleel, Aholiab, and "all that are wise hearted" the necessary gifts to construct the tabernacle. What implication does this passage have regarding government-imposed licensing laws, which serve to restrict entry of would-be competitors in various licensed professions? Licensing laws serve artificially to raise the incomes and social prestige of the favored licensed practitioners above what they would otherwise be able to enjoy in a truly competitive free-market situation. Such protective laws are simply bald attempts to benefit a privileged few at the expense of the unorganized many. Also, such licensing laws always come about by planned collusion between the professional practitioners who are seeking to be licensed and the civil authorities.[13] The push for licensing laws is often said to arise from the need to "protect the public from quacks." But this is nothing more than the argument presented by practitioners who desire the special benefits that licensing laws provide; it never comes from the general public, who always prefer a wide choice of service providers at low prices. Licensing laws effectively serve to squelch competition from would-be competitors by using the power of the state on behalf of the licensed profession.[14]

Question: Since every person is a unique, God-created individual with special gifts that can be applied in economic service to one's fellowmen, is it then proper for the civil authority to legally hinder the use of gifts that only God is capable of bestowing? Does not the civil authority that passes such protective legislation arrogate a power to itself that belongs only to God?

Question: Are there other workable alternatives to government-mandated licensing laws? Yes, but none that bestow such large benefits on those who are licensed. One alternative that would adequately protect consumers while still giving them wide choices at much lower costs is this simple solution: Let "licensing" be done by each competing professional organization, but *without* the coercive backing of the civil government! In short, let each professional group—and there might be a number of competing groups in each profession—grant "certificates of approval" to those practitioners who meet various criteria established by their own professional group. Then let each group advertise to the general public the advantages that are bestowed on consumers for choosing to do business with their members! This method is simple, fair to all concerned, and, best of all, *competitive*!

I used to write a weekly newspaper column with the by-line, "The competitive free-market is the workingman's best friend!" That, in my opinion, is an unchanging truth, as long as the civil authority fulfills its God-given role of maintaining a peaceful environment in which citizens are free to seek their own welfare and in which no one is allowed to use coercion on another. Most people are familiar with the Underwriters' "Seal of Approval." Consumers have come to trust this "Seal of Approval" because it has stood the test of time. The same procedure can be used in the non-government "licensing" I am describing here. Is it time to try it? I highly recommend doing so! Already-licensed professions would fight the idea to protect their own turf; but it would be a boon to consumers in the form of wider choices and much lower prices. Look what is happening as a result of more competition in the communications industry, the gas industry, and in the electrical energy industry. In each of these service is rising at rapid rates, and prices to consumers are falling!

Leviticus 19:17-18: God requires us to fear Him, to love Him, and to serve Him with our whole heart and soul, and to love our neighbor as ourselves. Thus, the application of economic enquiry must always be circumscribed and directed by God's law. This means that man-the-economist must continually delve into the Bible to make sure that he is always headed in the right direction; that is, that the economic ends man chooses to reach (a normative aspect of economics) are always in harmony with biblical precepts. Also, the mandate to love our neighbor seems to require that the study of economics be directed toward the end of *serving* our fellowmen rather than *manipulating* them to achieve our own self-centered ends. This is a quite-contrary perspective from that which most secularly oriented economic textbooks present, because they focus mainly on Keynesian-oriented manipulation to induce the population to meld in with government-induced monetary and fiscal policies. At least that is the major focus of secular economic texts in studying what is called *macro-economic* policy. In short, God's mandate to love our neighbor as ourselves would seem to indicate that all government attempts to macro-manage the economy to achieve nationally-established goals (which is nothing more than fascism in practice) is unbiblical.

These forbidden activities and agencies would include such things as taxing and spending to finance so-called "transfer payments" (Social Security, welfare, business and farm subsidies, etc.), wage and price controls, licensing professions, or any special legislation favoring one group over another. Also included are the numerous fascistic government-control agencies such as the Interstate Commerce Commission (ICC), the Federal Reserve Bank (FRB), the Federal Trade Commission (FTC), the Federal Communication Commission (FCC), the Food and Drug Administration (FDA), the Environmental Protection Agency (EPA), the Federal Emergency Management Agency (FEMA), and many, many others, too numerous to mention. All of the above-mentioned practices and agencies serve to build a fascistic centralized state similar to what existed in Mussolini's FASCIST Italy[15] and Hitler's NAZI Germany. They are all totalitarian in nature and threaten the freedom of American citizens. Most Americans have succumbed to decades of government propaganda, so they have wrongly come to believe that such evidences of fascism are a natural part of living in an advanced industrial and technological society, but nothing could be further from the truth.[16] Our challenge in this respect is to search the Scriptures to learn what God's word says about the limited role the civil authority is to play in society. Let us remember that only the biblical system of voluntary market exchange serves to maximize the outworking of true charity and service to others in any society, but especially in a society of free and self-responsible individuals before God.

Leviticus 19:35-36: Monetary inflation is immoral, whether it is effected by the government treasury *directly* printing fiat money, or whether it is brought about *indirectly* by the central bank (read: Federal Reserve Bank) insidiously "validating" government deficits through sophisticated forms of credit creation. Monetary inflation, which is properly defined as the creation of new purchasing media (money), is immoral because it insidiously changes the measure of the monetary unit by debauching the currency that people use in their every-day transactions. Monetary inflation is what counterfeiters engage in when they create false money, and it is just as morally wrong for civil rulers to "legally" create false money as it is for counterfeiters to do so illegally. In short, it is a clear breaking of God's admonishment to maintain a system of just weights and measures.

Garet Garrett, in writing about the Federal Reserve System and World War I, said:

> . . . after many years of blundering toward it, and only a few months before the beginning of the war in Europe [WWI], we had found the formula for the most efficient credit machine that was ever invented. This was the Federal Reserve System.[17]

We should evaluate this powerful, secret money-making machine in light of God's word and in light of a clear reading of the United States Constitution. At worst, it should be reconstructed; at best, it should be disbanded, for it constantly remains a threat to the people's liberty.

The Federal Reserve Bank has provided the needed sleight-of-hand credit financing to involve us in every foreign war during the 20th century and continues to do so in this new century. The net result of our getting involved in one foreign war after another has been a consequent steady decline in personal freedom; the growth of a highly centralized, bureaucratic and fascistic government; a horrendous rise in taxation; the planned destruction of the gold standard, which used to give some degree of protection to American citizens against an out-of-control, profligate, high- spending government in Washington, DC; and decades of planned monetary inflation which has brought the 1940 purchasing value of the dollar to less than 8 cents. Yes, 92 percent of the value of the 1940 dollar has evaporated as a result of the Federal Reserve's long-term inflationary monetary policy. The FRB has quietly cooperated (i.e., colluded) with the federal government to finance government deficits with readily supplied Federal Reserve credit.

Romans 13:1-8; I Timothy 2:1-2: The biblical role of civil government is simply to maintain law and order so that men can be free to pursue their legitimate economic interests in an atmosphere of peaceful service to God and their fellowmen.

When the civil authority goes beyond this very limited role by arrogating additional powers to itself, then it unlawfully invades other law spheres—the individual and home, the church, business firms and other voluntary organizations—and thereby it becomes tyrannical.[18]

In essence, the corporate state then becomes a secular god who will not allow any other law sphere to exist in freedom and independence. We are seeing this ugly face of atheistic humanism on the rise in our own American Republic, as well as throughout the world.

What Is to Be Done?

Only a return to a biblically-based concept of sphere law will be able to turn this ominous tide of social revolution. What people need to do is:

1) Study God's word to determine what the God-given role of civil government is in society. People who value freedom and who desire to remain free must rediscover the answer to this all-important question: What is the proper sphere of operation, and what are the legitimate biblical limitations to the power of civil rulers?

2) Study the United States Constitution and Bill of Rights to rediscover the clear limits of power that were so carefully delegated to the federal government by America's founding fathers.

3) Study their state constitution to understand how it also delegates and limits the power of the state.

In short, a good understanding of the historical setting which produced the Declaration of Independence, the Constitution of the United States, and your state is in order if needed changes in civil polity are to be wisely implemented. Also, it would be good to study the Anti-Federalist Papers to learn why certain Christian leaders like Patrick Henry opposed the Constitution of 1787 because it gave too much power to the central government.

The Bible speaks in many other ways to the study of economics and to the proper role of civil government (which is a closely related subject). Paul, in Chapter 12 of I Corinthians, speaks about the diversity of spiritual gifts in the church. This same principle, applied to economics, teaches us that the diversity of gifts which God has bestowed on mankind is what makes voluntary economic exchange between individual men, as well as between countries, profitable and beneficial to all participants. The Bible also instructs man to rest one day in seven. Fallen man might choose to work seven days and refuse to rest on the Sabbath, but God's word clearly says, "no." We should obey, first, for the very sake of obedience, but also because of trust that God loves us who are His creation and knows what is best for us.

In conclusion, let me briefly summarize what is clear. The Bible:

- provides us with a clear guide for economic development (Deut. 28) and limited civil government (Deut.17:14-20),

- stresses the dispersal of economic and political power in contrast to a concentration of power at the national or international levels (Gen.10:8-10, 11:1-9),

- focuses on the inseparable concepts of individual responsibility before God coupled with maximal personal economic freedom (Gen.1:26-28; Ex. 8:1), and

- insists that, because of man's innate sinful nature, mankind must rely on God's providence through free-market exchange, rather than trusting in the goodness of men, i.e., civil rulers (Jer.17:5,7,9,10; Ps.118:8-9).

Notes:

1 The "scientific method" is a thought process which involves five basic steps: 1) The searcher for truth collects empirical data. 2) Then the data are studied to discover uniformity to arrive at a generalization. 3) The searcher then forms an hypothesis, which explains the generalization. 4) Next, the hypothesis is tested through controlled experiments, thus producing a theory. 5) Lastly, the theory is applied by making predictions and then checking to see if it really works by producing truly predictable results. *See*: Tom Rose, Economics: Principles and Policy from a Christian Perspective, 2d ed. (Mercer, PA: American Enterprise Publications, 1987), 25.

2 Ibid., 27. 'Positive economics' is the so-called "pure science" aspect of economics which stresses the five-point thought process mentioned above. It focuses on the most efficient means of achieving pre-determined ends. 'Normative economics' is the broader aspect of economic study which deals with the ultimate ends and the directions toward which economic analysis is applied. Therefore, it involves the consideration of moral and ethical concepts.

3 *Theorem*: An idea that is demonstrably true, or assumed to be true.

4 *Theory*: Systematically organized knowledge applicable in a relatively wide variety of circumstances, especially a system of assumptions, accepted principles, and rules of procedure to analyze, predict, or otherwise explain a specified set of phenomena.

5 Economics: Principles and Policy from a Christian Perspective, 2d ed., and Economics: The American Economy from a Christian Perspective.

6 An economic application of this passage is that we as consumers should carefully read the labels of all processed foods. We should refrain from consuming those products which are too highly processed and thus have little real food value. We should also avoid

products that have been contaminated with unnatural preservatives used to extend shelf-life, thus actually becoming harmful to our bodies. So, over the years, the ingredients we use in making recipes have certainly changed!

7 *Precept*: A rule or principle imposing a standard of action or conduct.

8 *Insight*: The capacity to discern the true nature of a situation, an elucidating glimpse.

9 *a priori*: A preexisting viewpoint, which is largely determined by the world-and-life view that one holds.

10 Value exists *only* in a person's mind. To impute value is to mentally place a value onto: a *person* ("I love you"), an *object* (I like chocolate better than vanilla"), or an *available alternative* ("I'm going to choose this route instead of the other"). Man has the mental capacity of imputing value because God has shared this capability with man, who thus shares in this aspect of God's nature. For more information on the biblical application of value imputation, *See*: Tom Rose, Economics: Principles and Policy, 21, 22, 39, 44, 90-91, 99-100.

11 The biblical concept of sphere law teaches that each social sphere (the individual and family, the church, voluntary organizations, and the civil government) are *each* directly responsible to God, our Creator, who rules in every sphere. No sphere thus has the right to invade the responsibilities of another sphere. To do so would be to commit an act of gross tyranny. Note: The modern humanistic state (civil government) morally errs through the unbiblical process of arrogating unwarranted powers to itself and thereby invading the proper domain of other God-established law spheres. It is pertinent here to point out that, biblically, civil government is just one of various God-ordained social agencies. Civil government thus does *not* have open-ended power to do whatever civil rulers get a mind to do; but its rightful power is carefully limited by God's word. *See* Deuteronomy 17:14-20; I Timothy 2:1-2.

12 Virginia Commission on Constitutional Government, We The States: An Anthology of Historic Documents and Commentaries thereon, Expounding the State and Federal Relationship (Richmond, VA: The William Byrd Press, Inc., 1964), 150.

13 For a more thorough discussion of licensing laws and where pressures originate for them *See*: Tom Rose, "An Economic Analysis of Labor Unions," in Economics: The American Economy from a Christian Perspective (Mercer, PA: American Enterprise Publications, 1985), 20-24.

14 For those interested in this subject, look up information on the Flexner Report of 1910. One source is Douglass C. North and Roger LeRoy Miller, "The Economics of Rising Medical Costs," in The Economics of Public Issues, 6th ed. (New York: Harper & Row Publishers, 1983), 61-70.

15 The socialistic/fascistic state that Mussolini erected in Italy beginning in 1922 fascinated Franklin D. Roosevelt, who copied Mussolini's work when he fathered the National Recovery Administration in the early 1930s.

16 For a thorough discussion of the differences between socialism, fascism, and communism, *See*: Tom Rose, "The Isms," in Economics: The American Economy, 115-146.

17 Garet Garrett and Murray N. Rothbard, The Great Depression and New Deal Monetary Policy (San Francisco, CATO Institute, 1980), 5-6.

18 The fact that most citizens have been conditioned, mentally and morally, to accept such an expanded role of the civil government in society does not negate its inherent tyrannical nature.

The most efficient way of imposing tyranny on a population is to psychologically manipulate people, not only so they will tolerate, but that they will actually *embrace* the tyranny because they feel naked and exposed (as a result of their psychological conditioning) to the alleged dangers and demands of freedom if the tyrannical institutions were to be removed!

For centuries tyrants have realized that the easiest way to enslave a people is to make them fearful of accepting the many responsibilities that freedom daily demands of them as individuals. It is this fear of enduring the associated costs of freedom which continually feeds the humanistic drive for ever-increasing and ever-expanding the powers of centralized government.

II

Two Spheres of Action:
Voluntary (Free Market)
vs
Coercive (Civil Government)

3

THE FREE MARKET–ARGUMENTS
FOR AND AGAINST

But without thy mind would I do nothing; that thy benefit
should not be as it were of necessity, but willingly.
- Philemon 14

We live in a day and age when the institution of civil government in every nation in the world has become increasingly secular in its orientation and, therefore, has tended toward what the Old Testament regarded as Baal worship. In short, nations throughout the world have moved towards the practice of elevating civil rulers over their citizens so as to become secular "gods" that rule over and manipulate their citizens to achieve pre-determined socio/political/economic ends. The practical effect is a definite worldwide move towards socialistic/fascistic forms of political economies in which civil government increasingly regulates every aspect of human endeavor. We are called to apply God's word to the sphere of economics. It is the author's thesis that a systematic adherence to God's law will naturally and inescapably produce countries in which the power of civil government is carefully restricted, and that a blossoming of truly free-market economies will providentially occur in such a context. If a nation will submit to the Lordship of Christ, and its rulers will adhere to biblical law, then true freedom will flourish and economic prosperity will abound.

Nothing brings fear into the hearts of some people more quickly than mentioning the term "free market." Why is this so? One answer is that the general population has been so influenced mentally and emotionally by generations of socialist and pro-statist propaganda spewed from the news media, motion pictures, television programs, and false teaching emanating from slanted textbooks and ideologically leftward-leaning classroom teachers that very few people really understand what the free market is and how it operates. They have been led to believe, falsely, that rabid entities in a competitive free market system will voraciously prey on them as they stand helpless and unable to protect themselves or to effectively pursue their own economic self-interest. The solution to this alleged problem of free market economics is to flee to the "tender" protection of the political authority, whose proper role in society is, these fearful people are told, to protect helpless and unwary citizens from such avaricious plunderers as profit-seeking businessmen and entrepreneurs. "Put your trust in us," say the politicians and their appointed bureaucrats, "and we will devise a scheme of rules, regulations, and economic controls to protect you."

Let us consider this now widely accepted paradigm to see if it holds water.

First, let us admit that our world is indeed sinful and that it is full of individuals and organizations which stand ever-ready to take unfair advantage of the unwary. The number of thieves, robbers, liars, seducers, rapists, and unprincipled individuals and organizations abound! And any naive and ingenuous person who goes about life blissfully unaware of such threats to his economic well being is certain to be taken advantage of. But, is the solution to the always present problem of man's sinful nature really to be found in putting one's trust in the civil authority? The Bible warns us *not* to put our trust in princes (Ps.118:8 & 9, 146:3). And hard experience throughout history, and in our own day too, has shown that politicians, government bureaucrats, and even the judges of our courts, have sometimes proven themselves to be unworthy of trust. It is not at all unusual to learn that politicians have broken their pre-election promises, that bureaucrats have told outright lies, and that even Supreme Court Justices have rendered rulings that pervert the clear meaning of the U.S. Constitution. Evil is endemic to the world in which we live because of man's fallen nature. This is so regardless of the occupation or profession fallen men follow, and it also applies to civil rulers.

God Speaks to Man

God's word speaks to the issue of His law and in whom we are to put our trust:

> My son, forget not my law; but let thine heart keep my commandments:
> For length of days, and long life, and peace, shall they add to thee.
> Let not mercy and truth forsake thee: bind them about thy neck; write them upon the table of thine heart:
> So shalt thou find favor and good understanding in the sight of God and man. Trust in the Lord with all thine heart; and lean not unto thine own understanding.
> In all thy ways acknowledge him, and he shall direct thy paths.
> - Proverbs 3:1-6

> Keep my commandments, and live; and my law as the apple of thine eye.
> Bind them upon thy fingers, write them upon the table of thine heart.
> - Proverbs 7: 2-3

> A good man obtaineth favour of the Lord: but a man of wicked devices will he condemn.
> - Proverbs 12:2

> There is that maketh himself rich, yet hath nothing: there is that maketh himself poor, yet hath great riches.

Wealth gotten by vanity shall be diminished: but he that gathereth by labour shall increase.

- Proverbs 13: 7 & 11

Let every soul be subject unto the higher powers. For there is no power but of God: the powers that be are ordained of God.

For rulers are not a terror to good works, but to the evil. Wilt thou then not be afraid of the power? do that which is good, and thou shalt have praise of the same:

For he is the minister of God to thee for good. But if thou do that which is evil, be afraid; for he beareth not the sword in vain: for he is the minister of God, a revenger to execute wrath upon him that doeth evil. Wherefore ye must needs be subject, not only for wrath, but also for conscience sake.

- Romans 13:1, 3-5

It is better to trust in the Lord than to put confidence in man.

It is better to trust in the Lord than to put confidence in princes.

- Psalm 118: 8-9

Put not your trust in princes, nor in the son of man, in whom there is no help.

Happy is he that hath the God of Jacob for his help, whose hope is in the Lord his God:

Which made heaven, and earth, the sea, and all that therein is: which keepeth truth forever:

- Psalm 146: 3, 5-6

Man's Duty to God and to Man

Study the above verses carefully and prayerfully, for they deal with the crucial issues of: In whom should we place our trust without reservation and without question and whom should we trust only conditionally? Note that the verses also deal with the difficult subjects of when we should be properly subservient and obedient to the civil authority, and when we should not place our trust in mere mortal rulers.

First, we are told not to forget God's law, in essence, the Ten Commandments, and that doing so will add years to our life.

Next, we are told to hold on to mercy and truth (God's word is truth), that we should bind them around our neck and write them on our heart. In short, we are to be merciful and truthful in all that we do, and doing so will bring us the favor of both men and God. We are not to make our own man-made rules to live by, but we are to trust, with all our heart, in God and His rules. This is an unconditional command which applies to every aspect of life.

We are to keep God's commandments (which is often very difficult to do in a sinful world); and if we do so, we are promised blessings.

God blesses the good man and condemns the man of wicked devices, thus we are to express good will towards our fellowmen and to be of real service to them. In short, we are graciously to put the interest of others before our own.

Then we are reminded that wealth gotten by devious means will not be permanent or even be a blessing to us; but, happily and in contrast, wealth achieved by honest labor shall grow and be a blessing to the honest achiever.

The Need for Civil Government: Man's Tendency to Plunder Others

So far, the verses cited deal with our personal relationship with God as our Saviour and Lord, and with our personal relationship with our fellowmen. Now, if every person in society would stay properly attuned to God and His rules, and apply them faithfully in his daily life, all economic activity would then be beneficial and helpful to others. But realistically such is not the case. As Frederic Bastiat has stated:

Self-preservation and self-development are common aspirations among all people. And if everyone enjoyed the unrestricted use of his faculties and the free disposition of the fruits of his labor, social progress would be ceaseless, uninterrupted, and unfailing.

But there is also another tendency that is common among people. When they can, *they wish to live and prosper at the expense of others* (Italics added).[1]

For this reason, God has established civil government to protect against man's tendency to take unfair advantage of others and to live at their expense. In Romans 13 we are commanded to be subservient to those whom God has put in authority over us.

Note carefully two points: First, that this admonition to obey applies, not only to civil rulers, but also to parents, to church elders, to teachers, to employers, and to others who are in authority over us. Second, and this is very important, that God's admonition to obey those whom He has set over us is not an unqualified instruction to obey with blind obedience! The reason for this is very obvious. God Himself is the only power to whom we should give unquestioned and unqualified obedience; for only God Himself is worthy of such implicit faith, because only God is truly trustworthy in all that He says and does! God alone is truth, and all men are liars and unworthy of unquestioned trust because we are all burdened with the guilt of Adam's imputed sin.

Because of our fallen nature, we have an inherent tendency to plunder and take unfair advantage of our fellowmen. With authority comes power, and sinful man cannot be trusted to wield power over others unless such power is very carefully limited and restricted. This is accomplished by written constitutions (the Holy Bible, the constitutions of our various states and federal government, the constitutions and by-laws of voluntary organizations and business corporations, etc.).

The rightful power of civil rulers is limited to that of upholding God's law for the benefit of all those over whom they rule.[2] Thus they are "the ministers of God for good" and are, therefore, rightfully empowered with the authority of punishing evil doers, even to death, if necessary. Accordingly, we should fear rulers' power and obey their rightful mandates.

Ah, this is the problem! How are we to determine when to obey or not to obey the mandates of civil rulers? Theoretically, the answer is very simple: If a ruler's mandates are contrary to either God's law or to the written constitution of the state or federal government, then we are under no moral obligation to obey. We may sometimes, for the sake of prudence and our own immediate safety, wisely decide to obey even unconstitutional laws (which might possibly lead to the setting of dangerous, freedom-destroying precedents!). The reason for sometimes choosing to obey illegally imposed laws is that the ruler bears the sword and is in the frightful position of being able to use it unjustly, therefore the price to pay by ignoring the so-called law might at times be too great!

Furthermore, sometimes laws and regulations, when first promulgated, can appear unclear as to their biblical or legal basis and/or economic consequences. So, from a practical viewpoint, the answer to the question of when to obey or not to obey the edicts of civil rulers can often be cloudy and murky. The benefit of doubt, where doubt really exists, should always be given to those in authority because they have been put in their position by God and are, thereby, responsible directly to Him. But *never* are we allowed to forget that those in subjection owe their ultimate allegiance to God, who has left His infallible word, The Holy Bible, as our guide in every aspect of life.

There is one additional point we should always remember concerning the question of when to obey or not to obey those in positions of authority over us. It is this: Because of our own sinful natures, we have an innate tendency to be pulled in the direction of lawless rebellion rather than humble submission; so this is a caveat that we must always keep in mind, lest we serve to undermine rather than to build the Kingdom of God.

God's purpose in establishing civil government is to foster a climate of peace, godly freedom, and honesty so that man's individual freedom to act self-responsibly before God will be maximized. Such a climate of principled freedom greatly aids the widespread preaching of the Gospel of Christ. It also fosters the free and spontaneous economic interaction of men through mutually beneficial voluntary exchange.

The Blessings of Freedom

A spontaneous and dynamic increase in productive economic activity can be observed throughout the world in countries where civil rulers move from state-controlled economies towards free-market economies. Wherever such changes take place there is an immediate and beneficial increase in economic activity and a subsequent growth of productive wealth. The social process of free and self-responsible individuals interacting to their mutual advantage naturally occurs in a competitive marketplace in every society that is blessed with civil rulers who perform their God-given assignment of impartially maintaining law and order.

Old Testament Israel under the leadership of David, and to some extent under the leadership of Solomon, is a prime example of the economic blessings which can be expected in a country whose leaders rule according to God's law. Remember that Solomon later in his reign became tyrannical and laid heavy burdens on the people. This brought about a God-ordained act of governmental interposition led by Jeroboam and to the eventual splitting of the nation (I Ki. 11 & 12).[3]

The very rapid economic progress that occurred in these United States of America during the early years of our Republic is another example. Still another is the strong and prolonged economic development experienced by Japan as a result of the new and beneficial government policies instituted by General Douglas MacArthur in the post-World War II American occupation of Japan. MacArthur came to that war-torn country as a conquering military man, but left 13 years later as a beloved benefactor because of the godly policies he implemented. All these stand as examples of the beneficial economic effects enjoyed by nations whose rulers follow principles that are in conformity with biblical principles.

The beneficial process of spontaneous human interaction, to the mutual benefit of all parties concerned, occurs naturally because of each person's God-given bent to consistently seek the accumulation of wealth in the most economic (frugal) way. And this improvement in social progress and economic growth happens regardless of whether civil rulers are Christian or not. We have just mentioned the post-World War II economic progress of Japan under General MacArthur. More recently, observe the very rapid economic growth occurring in the Pacific rim countries that have been moving towards free-market practices and that respect and foster the right of citizens to own and control private property.

There can be no doubt that, if civil rulers implement laws that are in conformity with God's established law structure, beneficial economic and social effects will soon result. See, for instance, Deuteronomy 28:1-14 for a list of economic and social blessings that God promises to those peoples who adhere to His law. See verses 15-68 for a list of curses on those who do not. The real point to grasp from Deuteronomy 28 is that God will certainly bless those nations whose leaders turn to Him in faith and follow His revealed law. The blessings will be, most importantly, spiritual in nature, and then economic and social.

Note that the net effect, when the civil authority faithfully fulfills its proper role in society, is to maximize man's self-responsibility to God. For, in a free society where peace and safety truly reign, no other power can exist outside of the civil authority that can rightfully coerce any person to do other than follow his own free will.

But what about the freedom of evil men to do harm, for evil persons certainly do exist even in countries headed by godly rulers? This is why the civil authority is empowered by God to wield the sword. The ruler is to use lawful coercion to restrain evil! The rightful power of the civil authority is thus a negative force which is to be used for minimizing the potential outworking of man's evil heart in society. The civil ruler bears the sword, not for his own good or even for his own protection, but for the general benefit of the whole populace!

But What of Evil Men?

But, one might ask, in a free-market atmosphere won't evil men conspire with each other and thereby be free to maximize evil in society? The answer is no, not in a truly free market where competition exists and voluntarism truly reigns. First, we have God's institution of civil government which has the responsibility for punishing any person who wrongly imposes his will on another. This governmentally imposed restraint is exerted on both those of good intent, who might choose to use coercion to force their "good" ideas on others, as well as on those of evil intent, who might try to force others into submission. The existence of godly civil government creates a social atmosphere in which voluntary cooperation rather than coercive oppression is the norm. "A king that sitteth in the throne of judgment scattereth away all evil with his eyes" (Prov. 20:8).

It is true, of course, that civil rulers often fail in their responsibility to provide such an atmosphere, and we will consider this possibility shortly. Secondly, and perhaps even more importantly, God has instituted another deterrent to the general outworking of evil in society. He has done this by infusing a self-interested nature in man, and He has coupled this nature with man's inner (i.e., mental) ability to impute value. This empowers man with the ability, in an atmosphere of voluntarism, to base his outward actions upon his inner ranking of values. God has gifted man with some of God's own attributes, and thus man has the mental ability to make value imputations.

It works in this way: In an atmosphere of voluntary exchange, no person will knowingly act to the detriment of his or her own self-interest. Remember, it is the responsibility of the civil authority to establish a climate of peace in which lawful voluntary action will reign, thus enhancing man's self-responsibility to God. Remember also that the civil authority serves solely as a negative force in society to restrain evil and to punish those who are guilty of wrongly forcing others to act against their own will. In such a climate of voluntarism, the only way one person can get another to cooperate with him is to engage in the process of voluntary persuasion; this is sometimes called bartering or higgling and haggling. For instance, Joe will refuse to buy from or otherwise cooperate with Bill until he "sweetens the pot" sufficiently to induce Joe to acquiesce voluntarily to his wishes. This is what we might well call the *dynamics of voluntary action*, and it serves wondrously to restrain the outward working in society of man's evil heart. In this way, if the civil authority functions properly, and this is the crucial point, voluntarism reigns, and beneficial economic activity is thereby spontaneously generated throughout society.

Examples of "Legal Plunder"

A favorite author of mine, Frederick Bastiat, points out that law is the collective organization of the individual's right to lawful defense. He continues:

> Now since man is naturally inclined to avoid pain—and since labor is pain in itself—it follows that men will resort to plunder whenever plunder is easier than work. . . .
>
> It is evident, then, that the proper purpose of law is to use the power of its collective force to stop this fatal tendency to plunder instead of to work. All the measures of the law should protect property and punish plunder.[4]

Bastiat then points out that law is often perverted into a legal tool used to take property from one person or group and transfer it to others:

> . . . Sometimes the law places the whole apparatus of judges, police, prisons, and gendarmes at the service of the plunderers, and treats the victim—when he defends himself—as a criminal. In short, there is a *legal plunder*, . . .
>
> But how is this legal plunder to be identified? Quite simply. See if the law takes from some persons what belongs to them, and gives it to other persons to whom it does not belong. See if the law benefits one citizen at the expense of another by doing what the citizen himself cannot do without committing a crime.[5]

Thus, many of the harmful outworkings we find in society are the result of government power being misused. In what ways do we find civil authorities imposing economic burdens rather than fostering economic benefits? Here are a few key examples:

- Price controls such as minimum wages for workers or maximum prices that business people are allowed to charge consumers;

- Rent controls which limit the rents landlords can charge;

- Licensing laws that prohibit free entry of would-be competitors into various professions;

- Government subsidies to business firms, farmers, and to the poor and needy;

- Collusion between business leaders and civil rulers to establish monopolistic markets;

- Social security and Medicare programs, and many other examples of deceptive wealth-transfer schemes sponsored under government auspices.

The list could go on and on, but the examples given are sufficient. In every example there is sure to be a special-interest group that puts pressure on the civil authority to pass legislation or to promulgate rules and regulations which "feather their own nest" at the expense of others. Let us look at a few of the examples listed above:

Minimum Wage Laws and Price Controls: While many people seem to think that minimum-wage laws benefit all marginal workers by raising their pay, nothing could be further from the truth. The truth is that such laws harm the very marginal workers who are most at risk, and thus the most easily hurt. Who are these workers? They are the workers who are barely able to hold on to their jobs because, for one reason or another, they are not very productive. These are the first to be disemployed when the civil rulers raise their pay by official edict.

If a minimum wage of $5.00 per hour is good for baby sitters, why not raise the minimum wage to $10 or $15 per hour? If a minimum wage of $8.00 per hour is good for a marginal laborer (or a teenager, or anyone else), why not raise the wage to $20 per hour? The answer is evident: both mothers and employers will refuse to pay a wage above a certain level because the cost of paying exceeds the benefits received. They will turn to alternatives which disemploy those very persons whom the minimum-wage law was supposedly designed to help. The truth is that, even if man were not sinful, he is still finite, and thus he is severely limited, at any one time, in the information he is able to perceive and in the knowledge he can effectively assimilate and digest. No individual, nor any group of individuals, can be knowledgeable about all the factors that work synergistically to generate even one single market price. Thus no person, or group of persons, is able to determine for sure what the "correct" wage or price should be.

Government bureaucrats are especially subject to the human frailty of finiteness because they are rather insulated from the slow filtering of data from the marketplace. There are just too many economic fluctuations taking place at every moment of time in an economy containing millions of participating parties for the bureaucrats to be aware of them.

This inescapable fact about man's knowledge gap, that much information moves only slowly in society, and that it is highly subject to being perverted and twisted in the process of being transferred from one individual to another, and also likely to become intermixed with rumors and non-facts, provides ample reason for civil authorities to adopt a policy of non-interference with the free functioning of markets. A good biblical example is the instance when Benhadad, king of Syria, invaded Israel and besieged Samaria. The siege lasted so long that the price of food skyrocketed, but there is not the slightest indication that the king of Israel, Jehoram, imposed price controls. Even such an ungodly king as Jehoram did not presume to arrogate such unwarranted power to himself. Then Elisha prophesied, because of what God would do, that the price of food would drop precipitately the next day. (See II Ki. 6:24-7:20.)

Likewise, no ruling authority can know with certainty what the optimum level of wage is for each category of work in every market throughout the economy. Only God is capable of such knowledge, and for the civil authority to presume such capability for itself is nothing less than an attempt to set itself up as "God walking on earth." Georg Wilhelm Friedrich Hegel (1770-1831) regarded the state as the "Divine Idea" existing on earth, thus "God walking on earth." He viewed men as having *social* rights rather than *God-given* rights, and he viewed the state as the entity that prescribed rights and duties. For Hegel the state was the absolute power on earth; it was self-defining, sovereign, morally autonomous, and its subjects existed only through it and by it; and history alone was capable of judging it. This is a fearful picture of what many humanist-oriented nations under ungodly rulers have devolved into (including our own beloved Republic) as they have deviated from God's clear instructions that rulers are limited in power by the guidelines God has laid down in the Bible (See Deut.17:14-20).[6]

The result of civil authorities interfering with the free functioning of markets is always, and inescapably, an insidious transfer of wealth or the unfair granting of dangerous economic power to hidden special interests.

The "best" that the civil authority can do concerning an "optimum" minimum wage is never good enough. It is to make an "educated guess" at: what an optimum minimum wage might be, what its many inexorable consequences might also be, then to legally mandate that wage, and hope for the best. This is why the passage of minimum wage laws always has unanticipated hurtful effects on the very people the laws are supposedly designed to "protect." They help only those workers who happen to retain their jobs at the higher mandated wage, while they economically hurt those marginal workers who are subsequently disemployed because their productivity on the job is not sufficient to sustain the legally mandated wage.

It is interesting to note that, when businessmen set prices for the products and services they sell, they do so by making "educated guesses" as to how much consumers might be willing to pay, but usually only after conducting market surveys. But here is the difference between business-set pricing and bureaucratic-set pricing: If the businessman happens to err in judgment (which happens often), he quickly discovers his error through a drop in sales and an increase in inventory levels. Thus the businessman can quickly change his pricing before much damage occurs. Have you ever noticed how many times, when shopping, that you come across items marked down at special sale prices?

The government bureaucrat sitting in his secluded office, though, only finds out belatedly that the government has erred in setting a price that conflicts with what is really happening in the marketplace. And this happens only after the erroneous price has had a wide and harmful impact throughout the economy. Even after the long-delayed discovery has been made, the political edict can only with difficulty be changed because the government bureaucrat and his political bosses must then contend with the various special-interest groups who benefit from the politically mandated price! As we see then, businessmen have a strong economic incentive to *correct* their mistakes relatively quickly, but government bureaucrats and politicians have strong political reasons to resist making needed changes.

Why, then, do politicians persist in passing minimum wage laws? Because the world runs, not on reality, but on the perception of reality, and the majority of the public has been erroneously led to believe that minimum wage laws do indeed "protect" marginally productive workers. Few people really understand how free market principles actually work to protect ordinary workers from being oppressed, nor do they understand the political incentives that constantly beckon demagogues to succumb to special-interest groups which are always lobbying behind the scenes in the halls of our state legislatures and national government. The end result is that we get politically mandated economic restrictions that are purported to "help" one segment of society or another, but what we actually get in reality is a rearranging of the playing field to benefit only certain special-interest groups.

There are tens of thousands of lobbyists employed in our nation's capital by business firms, labor unions, political action committees, and other special-interest groups. Representative Dick Armey recently stated that the number of lobbyists in Washington, D.C., rose from about 20,000 to almost 70,000 between 1964 and 1993, and that the increasing number closely tracked the increasing complexity of the federal tax code.[7] Charles Lewis of the Center for Public Integrity, a watchdog group, pointed out:

> As long as you have the most powerful, influential city in the world here and also the most lucrative market in the world, and as long as you have a trillion-and-a-half-dollar budget, Washington is going to be center stage for influence peddling.[8]

With reference to influence peddling, Rep. Armey stated that Congress has a vested interest in keeping the tax code complex because lobbyists bear gifts in the form of campaign cash.[9]

To the number of lobbyists cited above add those employed similarly in our state capitals and in our many, many city halls and county courthouses. This will give the reader only a slight idea of the hidden manipulators who are constantly attempting, either to alter market forces through the power that civil rulers wield, or to protect themselves from market alterations previously caused by other behind-the-scenes manipulators. It must be noted here that, once one group is able to skew things in its favor, this generates an excuse, and sometimes even a legitimate need, for other parties to rush into the legislative halls to protect their own economic interests. For others it creates an opportunity to join in the political process of commandeering their own piece of the economic pie that is being subtly, but forcefully, redistributed by legislative fiat. The whole process of political intervention in the marketplace soon begins to feed on itself in a never-ending contest for gaining political influence. The only sure defense against creating such a nightmarish arena of conflicting special interests is to ask the question: *"From a biblical standpoint, what is the proper role of civil government in society?"*

One unwholesome but inescapable outcome of this scenario is that citizens come to look upon the power wielded by civil authorities as something they can enlist for their own economic advantage. Under-the-table payments inevitably come into play, as do other forms of bribery and corruption; but, even more importantly, a growing tendency is generated for everyone involved to place ever-increasing power in the hands of civil rulers to distribute the largess that Frederic Bastiat correctly designated "legal plunder."

The result of this whole process becomes an economy dominated by political influence in which a new type of individual rises to positions of power and influence. It is no longer the forward-looking entrepreneur or the hard-working successful businessman, but the person peculiarly skilled in political machination who becomes the major influence in society. Slowly, a once-free-market economy is imperceptibly changed into a socialist/fascist type of centrally controlled economy in which bureaucratic rulers continually manipulate citizens and one sector of the populace or another for the benefit of their favored "politically correct" friends.

Licensing Laws: Modern Americans have become so acclimated to accepting licensing laws without question that they fail to realize the extent to which such laws have been used to extort additional money from the public under the guise of "protecting consumers from quacks." How did this come about?

To answer this question we turn to the first decade of the 1900s when there were 192 medical schools in these United States. In 1910 the Carnegie Foundation commissioned Abraham Flexner to inspect the existing medical educational facilities in our country. At that time the leaders of the American Medical Association felt that there was an over-supply of medical practitioners. The result of the Flexner Report was a drastic decrease in the number of medical schools which served as the source for supplying new physicians. By 1944 the number of medical schools had dropped from 192 to 69. The number of physicians per 100,000 population, as a result of the drastic reduction in the number of medical schools, dropped from 157 in 1900 to 132 in 1957.[10]

The reason for this great drop in the number of physicians can be explained by the tight control the American Medical Association exerted, and continues to exert, on the accreditation of medical schools, and thus the potential supply of new medical practitioners allowed into the lucrative medical field. As older doctors retired or died, they were not replaced by a sufficient number of new entrants. That this is exactly what the AMA hoped for was reported in 1928 by the former head of the AMA's Council on Medical Education:

> . . . the reduction of the number of medical schools from 160 to 80 (resulted in) a marked reduction in number of medical students and medical graduates. We had anticipated this and felt that this was a desirable thing. We had . . . a great oversupply of poor and mediocre practitioners.[11]

Be careful to note that his statement about having "a great oversupply of mediocre practitioners" was nothing more than a partisan value judgment. Note also that the market-interfering action of the AMA was purposely designed to limit only the *future supply* of new practitioners. It did absolutely nothing to evaluate the *qualifications* of the then-existing practitioners, nor the qualifications of new graduates who emanated from the lower number of accredited medical schools.

The net economic effect of licensing practitioners in any field is to restrict the number of new entrants, thus limiting supply and boosting average incomes. This assured effect of licensing explains why practitioners in so many professions and occupations go to the civil authorities and lobby for licensing laws. Recently, in the State of New York, licensed hair dressers requested the licensing authority to take action against a 14 year-old Negro girl who had worked up a good business by braiding the hair of other young Negro girls. The licensing board claimed its action was to "protect" members of the public who might be "harmed" by the unlicensed young lady.[12]

This same plea of "protecting the public" is used by all licensed professions that the author is aware of. Another attack was recently made by a dental association on dental technicians who had set up their own practices of providing teeth cleaning services. Again, the claim of the licensed practitioners was that the health of the public might be endangered if dental assistants were allowed to practice without being under the direct supervision of a licensed dentist. Note that such actions by licensed professionals to allegedly "protect the public welfare" uniformly end up at one predetermined goal: They invariably deny the public freedom to choose between lower-cost providers and higher-cost providers. The net result is to remove the low-cost providers for the benefit of the higher-cost providers, at the expense of the public!

Licensing laws use the police power of civil government to prevent consumers from employing the professional services of those they prefer, usually lower-cost providers. Instead, the only options left open to consumers is either to do without, or to pay the higher price demanded by the licensed practitioner. The supporting assumption behind all licensing laws is that members of the public are not generally intelligent enough to decide what is in their own best interest, therefore they must be "protected" by a coalition of the licensed practitioners and the civil power. This is true whether those who claim they are protecting the public interest are plumbers, electricians, hair dressers, auto mechanics, attorneys, dentists, medical doctors, or any other licensed group.

Some years ago the Chinese practice of acupuncture, a profession that has existed for almost 2,000 years in China without any type of legal supervision, became popular in our country. It grew in popularity because members of the public could see and experience positive benefits from acupuncture. American physicians responded to this alternative health-inducing therapy by seeking a free-market response—they sought training from the real experts in that field, the Chinese acupuncturists themselves. But, once a goodly number of physicians were trained, it was not long until the American Medical Association sought legislation that would require non-licensed acupuncturists to work under the supervision of licensed medical doctors, who had themselves just recently learned the skill! And so the story goes!

In short, the fundamental issue behind the licensing of professions turns out to be, not the *protection of the public* but simply a *turf battle* to protect the narrow economic interest of one group of practitioners from would-be competitors.

The free-market solution to such a perceived "problem" is simply to allow consumers to decide for themselves who provides the best service at an agreeable price. In a free society should not any person who wishes to provide a good or service be allowed to do so, as long as no deception is involved? Damages resulting from services based on deceptive practices are recoverable in courts of law. Throughout history the potential threat of malpractitioners being sued for damages has been a sufficient deterrent to protect the public.

The public would receive additional protection from incompetent practitioners if each profession advertised its products and services to "enlighten" consumers as to why their interest would be best served by choosing one provider over another. In this way consumers would themselves be empowered to make a more intelligent choice. Such an approach would provide a level playing field for all contestants, and it would leave would-be-practitioners a wide choice of how to seek adequate training to enter a profession (attending school, serving as an understudy to a successful practitioner, etc.), and all this without a narrower selection of choices being forced on the public by governmental edict.

The medical profession in America (as well as in some other countries) provides perhaps the most auspicious example of how licensing laws serve to protect the narrow economic interest of licensed practitioners. That is why we choose this particular profession as the prime example of the effects of licensing laws, and not because the author has any particular ax to grind against medical doctors as such. It just happens that the licensing wall of protection built around the medical profession, and the educational propaganda programs supporting widespread public acceptance of such "protection," is much further advanced in medicine than in most other professions.

Some years ago, a medical doctor who was a professor at a university in Washington, D.C., delivered a very interesting address to graduating medical technologists at the University of Texas Medical School in Dallas, Texas. In his talk, Dr. P—— told graduates that pressure for licensing always comes from within the ranks of groups who seek protection from others that compete with them. He also pointed out that the goal of licensing is not to "protect the public, but that such laws raise the prestige and incomes of those in the licensed professions." He told the graduates that the practice of licensing began over 100 years ago out of *self*-interest rather than for the public good.

This author happened to be sitting in the audience because he had a daughter who was among the graduating seniors. I took careful notes and later wrote to the doctor, stating that he had spoken of things in his address that I had been teaching in my college economics classes for many years, and I asked if I could quote him. His reply is of interest:

> I am, of course, flattered that you recall my remarks. . . .
>
> I was not speaking so much of physicians and dentists who have been universally licensed for more than a century, but of the newer health occupations that seek licensing and/or certification and/or hospital regulations as devices for 1) enhancing professional prestige, and 2) restricting scope of practice. I suppose that, derivatively, these goals could tend to enhance income, but I don't believe that increased income is the conscious primary motivation. . . .
>
> . . . A hospital licensure bill currently before the City Council (District of Columbia) would require hospitals to grant staff privileges to nurse midwives, psychologists, and several other categories of independent practitioners. It has sent the Medical Society into a tizzy. . . .
>
> . . . In summary, I would say that "licensure" is not the only mechanism that occupations use to "protect territory" and enhance prestige. While higher income is not usually the primary motivation, I won't deny that it often has that effect. . . .[13]

Incomes in the medical field have risen rapidly since the licensing and accrediting of medical schools under the auspices of the American Medical Association. North and Miller report that: 1) while consumer prices rose 280 percent between 1950 and 1980, the medical care index increased by 350 percent; 2) in 1970 physicians had the highest average income of any profession at $41,000, compared to non-licensed professions like engineers at $17,700, and full college professors at $16,800.[14]

The Federal Reserve Bank of St. Louis reports that medical care prices have for a long time risen faster than the widely quoted Consumer Price Index. From January, 1957, to June, 1992, medical care prices rose 6.7 percent annually, versus 4.6 percent for the CPI less medical care.[15]

Since most people have difficulty grasping just how much difference a few percentage points per year make over a period of time, note the graph below which shows how much more rapidly the Consumer Price Index, *including* medical care, has risen in comparison to the Consumer Price Index, *less* medical care.[16]

CPI for Medical Care and CPI Less Medical Care

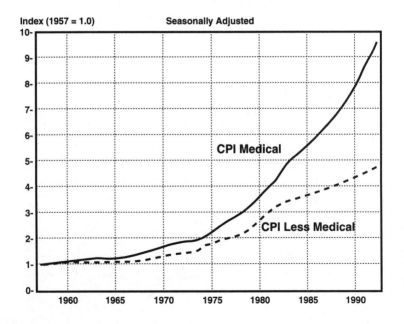

Note that for the period shown the CPI, *less* medical care, has risen from an index of one to just under five; while the CPI, *including* medical care, has risen from an index of one to just under twelve. In short, the total increase for medical prices (which are costs to consumers) has more than doubled between 1957 and 1992. This indicates a tremendous diversion of consumers' resources being siphoned off to a special-interest group because of licensing laws which insulate the medical profession from competition that would otherwise exist in a free-market scenario.

This same sort of monetary diversion accomplished by the coercive power of civil government is enjoyed by every other special-interest group that is protected by licensing laws. It is interesting to note here that militant labor unions sometimes attempt to squelch competition presented by non-union workers by resorting to threats or the actual use of physical violence, which is illegal. But licensed professions take a much more effective and sophisticated means to achieve much the same end; they simply pick up the phone and notify the licensing authority, which then applies the police power of the civil government to remove would-be competitors from the market.

The years of required schooling for physicians has also been greatly lengthened, and this serves as an added barrier to entry. In addition, the number of students allowed to enroll in medical schools has been greatly restricted, as many qualified prospective students who have been denied entry can readily substantiate. All this has occurred under the guise of "improving the quality of service" for the "good of the public." The substantially higher income flowing to licensed practitioners in the protected system is seldom viewed by them as the main reason for restricting the number of new entrants. Consumers, however, remain unconvinced because they are the ones who pay the higher costs. These additional costs fall on consumers in two ways: first, in paying higher fees to the licensed practitioners and, second, in the longer amount of time spent waiting at the practitioners' office.

In summary, the supply of medical practitioners has been drastically curtailed both because of the accreditation of medical schools and the licensing of practitioners. The demand for medical services, on the other hand, has increased greatly because of such things as Medicare and Medicaid, third-party payment systems like health insurance, and laws that make it very difficult, if not impossible, for the consuming public to legally order simple laboratory tests or widely used drugs and medicines without first having to go to a licensed medical practitioner to obtain prescriptions. In addition, the FDA has been threatening to drastically limit consumers' access to herbal remedies (which cannot be patented because they are natural substances).

All of these factors serve either to decrease the supply of medical practitioners available to the public or to artificially add to the demand for their services. Add to this the ubiquitous "educational propaganda" programs constantly aimed at the public through the news media to dissuade people from taking primary responsibility for their own health—that they should never do anything without first seeking advice from their medical advisor—and we end up with an easily malleable populace who run to their licensed practitioner for every petty ailment. The end result is that the general public has very little awareness of alternative treatments, or much sensitivity of the direct costs involved, because of the widespread existence of third-party payers like insurance companies and government agencies.

Third-party payment practices serve to insulate seekers of medical services from the immediate economic "pain" of feeling the financial pinch of increased medical costs at the point of purchase. Restrictive licensing practices (i.e., the accreditation of medical schools and licensing of doctors, and legally requiring consumers to go through licensed medical doctors to order laboratory tests and prescription medicines) serve to force members of the public into a tightly controlled channel of medical products and services. This tightly controlled institutional framework quietly, but firmly, denies consumers ready access to potentially better and lower-cost services. This all occurs without one person in a thousand being aware of how the public is being manipulated for the benefit of an enormously profitable special-interest group.

Historical Examples of Suppressing Competition

The licensed medical profession has a long history of vigorously suppressing both licensed and unlicensed practitioners who persist in offering suffering people alternative methods of treatment (i.e., methods of recovering health which have not been "officially" approved or endorsed by the American Medical Association or the Food and Drug Administration). Here are a few individuals who successfully treated people for cancer—who had been given up as hopeless by the licensed medical profession—that were persecuted for following "non-approved" methods of cure:

Rene Caisse, a nurse in Canada, was given an herbal formula in1922 by an Ojibwa Indian for curing cancer. She used this formula successfully until she died in 1978. She had an 80% cure rate for patients whom the standard medical practitioners had sent home to die. She was persecuted and harassed in Canada. Caisse then moved to New York where she continued her life-saving services under the umbrella of protection afforded by a sympathetic licensed practitioner, Charles Brusch, M.D., of the Brusch Medical Center, Cambridge, Massachusetts. Brusch published a notarized statement on April 6, 1990, stating he had cured his own cancer by sole use of "Essiac" (Caisse spelled backwards), the name given to the formula.[17]

Royal Raymond Rife was a brilliant researcher and inventor. In 1933 he developed a super-powerful microscope that magnified by 60,000 times and which had a resolution of 31,000. Using his microscope he was able to observe live bacteria and viruses in action, something that had never been done before. By observation he discovered that each living organism oscillated at a specific rate, and he theorized that he might be able to kill harmful organisms by zeroing in on them at their specific mortal-oscillation rate if he could develop a machine to do so. Soon he was successfully treating cancer patients by focusing his newly invented "beam machine," or "Rife Generator," on cancerous tumors. Unlike modern x-ray therapy, the rays from his machine did not destroy healthy tissue along with cancerous tissue.

Rife used his electronic generator to successfully treat many cancer patients as well as patients suffering from other diseases. His work of curing 14 of 16 terminal cancer patients within a three-month period was well observed and carefully documented by the Special Research Committee of the University of Southern California clinic under the direct supervision of Milbank Johnson, M.D., chairman of the committee. Rife worked in close collaboration with other leading medical researchers of that time, but the low cost and high effectiveness of treatment by using his microscope and Rife generator conflicted with already-accepted, more costly procedures. Richard Walters reports:

> But Rife's lifesaving medical technology never reached the American people. His work threatened powerful doctors and financial interests. . . . the Rife generator was seen as a direct competitive threat to the big drug companies, surgeons, doctors, health bureaucracies, and other vested interests. As Barry Lynes shows in his dramatic, well-documented book *The Cancer Cure That Worked*, the American Medical Association, with the California State Board of Public Health, launched a systematic campaign to destroy Rife and his therapy. By 1939, the AMA virtually stopped the Rife treatment by harassing physicians and threatening them with loss of license and jail terms and by forcing Rife into court. All scientific reports on Rife's work were censored by the head of the AMA; no major medical journal was permitted to report on Rife's medical discoveries and cures.
>
> Doctors who used the Rife instrument were visited by officials and harassed. Any doctor who made use of Rife's methods was stripped of his privileges as a member of the local medical society. . . .[18]

Gaston Naessens, a French biologist who now lives in Canada, developed a non-toxic cure for cancer called 714-X. A few years ago the news media reported about a teen-age boy from New England, Billy Best, who ran away from home because he no longer wanted to undergo chemotherapy and the terrible side effects of the treatments. He finally agreed to return home when promised that he would not have to undergo more chemotherapy. He then was allowed to take 714-X and was soon cured. 714-X is a nitrogen-enriched camphor solution. Naessens, in spite of the success of his discovery, has been harassed by the Canadian medical authorities.

Stanislaw Burzynski, M.D., practices medicine in Houston, Texas, where he is harassed by the AMA and the FDA. He discovered that a group of peptides, which are short chains of amino acids, and which naturally occur in our bodies, inhibit cancerous cell growth. Using this knowledge, he developed a treatment that has been successful in curing cancer in advanced stages in thousands of patients. The news media in 1996 showed news clips of people demonstrating in support of Dr. Burzynski when the FDA temporarily closed down his clinic. For 13 years the FDA persecuted Dr. Burzynski because of his successful and innovative procedures in fighting cancer. The FDA raided his clinic and confiscated the medical files of his patients. Such strong-arm tactics are not at all unusual in the attempts by medical authorities to squelch "unapproved" methods of treatment which threaten "approved" but relatively unsuccessful establishment practices.

Harry Hoxsey's great-grandfather had a horse that developed cancer. He put the horse in a pasture and noted that the horse ate certain herbs which soon effected a cure. So the grandfather started offering these herbs to cure humans of cancer. The formula was passed through the family on to Harry on condition that he would not charge people for the herbs. Harry complied and, because oil was found on his Texas property, he was financially able to set up a clinic in Dallas in 1924. Many people were successfully treated, but the medical establishment attacked and had him arrested many times for practicing medicine without a license.

In 1954 an independent team of ten physicians made a two-day inspection of Hoxsey's clinic and stated that Hoxsey was "successfully treating pathologically proven cases of cancer, both internal and external, without the use of surgery, radium or x-ray." The team went on to report that a sufficient number of cases had remained free of symptoms in excess of five to six years, and some for as long as 24 years, and that all were enjoying exceptional health. In spite of this excellent report, the AMA continued its attack on Hoxsey. In 1953, the Fitzgerald Report, which was commissioned by the U.S. Senate, concluded that organized medicine had conspired to suppress the Hoxsey therapy and at least a dozen other promising cancer treatments.

Legal Plunder

Again, please note that we chose to evaluate the economic impact of licensing in the medical profession, not because we don't appreciate the many dedicated and talented practitioners within that noble profession, but simply because the medical profession has been eminently more successful in raising practitioners' incomes at the expense of the general public (even more successful than the law profession). The very same investigation and economic analysis can be made for other professions, many of which are even now striving to emulate the great monetary success of the medical profession by following the same strategy. Knowledge of how one special-interest group has benefitted itself at the expense of the general public has empowered other special-interest groups to emulate the medical profession. But the general public must be made aware of how *all* licensing laws amount to a form of legalized theft.

The public needs to understand that licensing laws impose heavy economic burdens on the very people who are least able to protect themselves against the resulting increased costs: the poor, the unlearned, and the majority of citizens who don't have the needed political connections to engage in behind-the-scenes machinations that go on in the halls of our state and national legislatures (See Eph. 6:12). The result is that what should be the legitimate powers of the civil authority are turned into a subtle but difficult-to-recognize engine of legalized plunder.

Frederic Bastiat masterfully addresses how the law can be and often is perverted to turn it into a tool of plunder for special-interest groups:

> The law perverted! And the police powers of the state perverted along with it! The law, I say, not only turned from its proper purpose but made to follow an entirely contrary purpose! The law become the weapon of every kind of greed! Instead of checking crime, the law itself guilty of the evils it is supposed to punish! If this is true, it is a serious fact, and moral duty requires me to call the attention of my fellow-citizens to it.[19]

Now let us turn to an interesting example from early American history of how a special-interest group used its influence to protect itself from competition. The time is the early 1760s, just after what is known as the French and Indian War in America, but as The Seven Years' War in Europe. The English and the American colonists were able to expel the French from Canada and the Ohio Valley territory, a lush piece of real estate into which the American colonists were increasingly pouring over the Appalachian Mountains to settle as traders, hunters, and farmers. The problem caused by the flow of newcomers was that their presence upset the Indian tribes who understandably resisted the influx of immigrants into their territory. But, even more important to the civil rulers of the time was that the continued influx of colonial traders who came *with* the settlers created unwanted competition for the monied interests in London.

To solve this competitive threat the English Parliament passed the Proclamation of 1763, which absolutely prohibited settlement in the Ohio valley west of the Appalachian divide. Benjamin Franklin, who was then representing the American Colonies in England, delivered the following address to the British House of Commons in 1766. He spoke of the Proclamation of 1763 as a yoke that was placed about the neck of the colonists solely on the basis of economics because of the value of the Indian trade to the London traders.

The trade with the Indians, though carried on in America, is not an American interest. The people of America are chiefly farmers and planters; scarce anything they raise or produce is an article of commerce with the Indians. The Indian trade is a British interest: it is carried on with British manufacturers, for the profit of British merchants and manufacturers.[20]

We include this example simply to show that special-interest groups have for centuries pressured civil rulers to eliminate would-be competitors. Still earlier examples can be discovered by studying the histories of ancient Rome, ancient Greece, and other ancient civilizations.

A Modern Example of Gaining Monopoly Power

Now let us turn to an up-to-date example that has to do with the alleged threat of destroying the ozone layer in the earth's stratosphere. Since December 1, 1995, federal law has banned the use of chloroflourocarbons (CFCs) in these United States. Why is this so, and how did it come about? The answer is that, for some years now, a campaign has been waged by environmentalists to ban CFCs because they claim that leakage into the atmosphere of CFCs, which include Freon (or R-12, as it is commercially known), supposedly destroys the ozone layer in the atmosphere that protects people from skin cancer. DuPont held the patent for Freon (R-12) which expired in 1992. But here the plot thickens. It "just so happens" that DuPont has developed a *new* refrigerant called SUVA 134a for which it presently holds the patent! Eric Peters writes that it was DuPont that was secretly behind the environmentalists' and media's push to outlaw Freon:

> But with the patents on Freon running out in 1992, DuPont faced the prospect of losing millions annually as competitors entered the Freon market, in the United States and abroad. About this time we began to hear hysterical shrieks about an "ozone hole" and

the "dangers" of man-made chloroflourocarbons (CFCs) like Freon.

The argument, in its essentials, held that leakage of Freon from automobile air conditioners and other sources was allowing chlorine molecules to escape and make their way into the upper atmosphere where they would deplete the ozone layer, creating a "hole."
. . .

. . . the theory was accepted uncritically by the media, which peddled it in alarming tones. . . .

Shortly thereafter, a U.N. Treaty (the Montreal Protocol) was signed that called for the gradual phase-out of all CFC-based refrigerants. . . .[21]

Bill Kramer points out that ozone fluctuations in the atmosphere are extremely complex because they are subject to many variables, including changes in solar activity, volcanic eruptions, and even climate variations due to ocean currents. He states that ozone fluctuates naturally from season to season and place to place, but that average levels have remained essentially the same.[22]

Knowledgeable scientists have discredited the ozone scare, but the scare has served the special economic interest of one specific company that was apparently very successful in hyping the environmental groups and the media to bring about favorable legislation which ensures its receiving high profits on a new patent that has years to run. The replacement refrigerant SUVA is much more expensive and reportedly *many times more threatening* to the atmosphere than Freon. The Freon scare serves as an instructive lesson of harmful governmental intrusion in the marketplace that benefits a special-interest company that lurked behind the scenes, and it serves as a warning to consumers to beware of possible hidden influences behind government's attempts to "protect the public."

The thesis held by the author is this: If civil rulers can be brought to adhere to biblical law and the Constitution of these United States, then true freedom and self-responsibility before God will be maximized. In such a climate the ability of special-interest groups to live at the expense of others ("legalized theft") will be minimized and the outworking of the true free market will be enhanced to the general benefit of consumers.

Notes:

1 Frederic Bastiat, *The Law* (NY: Irvington-on-Hudson, The Foundation for Economic Education, 1962), 9.

2 This is why we are admonished by God's Word to pray for those who rule over us (See I Tim. 2:1 & 2), "That we may lead a quiet and peaceable life in all godliness and honesty."

3 For a detailed biblical and historical account of governmental interposition, See: Tom Rose, *Reclaiming the American Dream By Reconstructing the American Republic* (Mercer, PA: American Enterprise Publications, 1996).

4 Bastiat, *The Law*, 10.

5 Ibid., 20-21.

6 C. Gregg Singer, *From Rationalism to Irrationality: The Decline of the Western Mind from the Renaissance to the Present* (Phillipsburg, NJ: Presbyterian and Reformed Publishing Company, 1979), 113-114; and Eugene Weber, *A Modern History of Europe* (New York: W. W. Norton & Company, 1971), 662.

7 John Merline, "Cutting the Lobbyists' Influence," *Investor's Business Daily*, 30 (July 1996), 1.

8 Ibid.

9 Ibid., 2 (A).

10 Douglass C. North and Roger LeRoy Miller, *The Economics of Public Issues* (New York: Harper & Row, 1983), 63.

11 Ibid., 63.

12 The reader can determine in his own mind whose interest the licensed practitioners were really seeking.

13 Tom Rose, *Economics: The American Economy* (Mercer, PA: American Enterprise Publications, 1985), 22-23.

14 North & Miller, *The Economics of Public Issues*, 61, 63.

15 Kevin L. Kliesen, "Medical Care Price Increases: A Long-Running Story," *National Economic Trends* (August 1992), 1.

16 Ibid.

17 Richard Thomas, <u>The Essiac Report</u> (Los Angeles: Alternative Treatment Information Network, 1993).

18 Richard Walters, <u>Options: The Alternative Cancer Therapy Book</u> (Garden City Park, NY: Avery Publishing Group, 1993), 271. The material in this and the following examples is taken from this book and from information in the author's personal files.

19 Bastiat, 5.

20 Allan W. Eckert, <u>That Dark and Bloody River: Chronicles of the Ohio River Valley</u> (New York: Bantam Books, 1955) 653, fn 103.

21 Eric Peters, "Who's Behind the Freon Ban?," <u>The Free Market</u> (December 1996): 6.

22 Bill Kramer, "American Military Is Jeopardized By An International Ban On CFCs," <u>The Spotlight</u>, 16 December 1996, 14-15.

4

THE BLESSINGS AND CURSES
OF CIVIL GOVERNMENT

... it shall come to pass, if thou shalt hearken
diligently unto the voice of the Lord thy God, ...
... all these blessings shall come on thee, ...
But ... if thou wilt not hearken unto the voice
of the Lord thy God,
... all these curses shall come upon thee, ...
– Deuteronomy 28:1-2, 15

A recent study of 75 countries[1] shows a strong correlation between the standard of living enjoyed by a people and the degree of bureaucratic red tape that is required by their civil government before a business firm is allowed to start doing business in the marketplace. The study showed that the richer, more affluent countries provide relatively easier and less-costly entry barriers while the poorer, less-developed countries (LDCs) erect more time-consuming costly barriers for starting a business. A sampling of government requirements from the 75 countries surveyed showed various country-by-country contrasts from which we can draw some very helpful insights. The governmental requirements to do business in each country were divided into three categories:

1. The number of legal procedures that are required to start doing business.

2. The number of days needed to go through the various legal procedures.

3. The total financial outlay of all out-of-pocket costs for licenses and other fees. To make comparisons meaningful between various countries with drastically differing standards of living, this category was measured as a percentage of each country's per-capita Gross Domestic Production (GDP). (I will explain this through some examples shown below.)

First, let us look at the average data for all 75 countries surveyed:

1. The average number of mandated legal procedures for the 75 countries was 10. That is, each aspiring business entrepreneur, on average, had to progress through ten separate steps to gain governmental approval to legally open the doors of his business.

2. The average number of days required to go through the mandated steps for the 75 countries was 63 days.

3. The average per-capita financial outlay in all countries to progress through the various legal hoops was 34 percent of GDP. To explain: The figure of 34% for the 75 countries surveyed means that the financial outlay to legally start a business uses up, on average, more than one-third (34%) of the total annual value of domestic goods and services produced by one person. In other words, a figure of 100% would mean that all the required legal hoops cost a full year of one person's economic output. Thus, a figure of 34% means that the total legal cost is over 4 months of one person's total GDP! Of course, in many countries there are also numerous off-the-book bribes and under-the-table payments that are customarily paid before getting a legal go-ahead to start a business.

Rich Country, Poor Country

Now that we understand what the *average* figures are, let's look at some individual countries for the purpose of drawing comparisons:

- Canada has the fewest legal procedures required and the fewest number of days needed, at two for each.
- Bolivia has the most legal procedures required, at 20.
- Mozambique, at 174 days, needs the longest time to get all the legal procedures approved; a wait of almost six months!
- Egypt has the greatest total entry cost as a percentage of per-capita GDP, at 216%. What this means is that a business entrepreneur in Egypt has to endure a cost of *more than two years* of a person's GDP to legally start a business!
- New Zealand has the lowest percentage cost of GDP for starting a business, at 4/10 of one percent.

It is instructive to note that the *richest* (most economically developed) countries in the world have the *lowest* percentage cost of per-capita GDP for legally starting a new business. In contrast, the *poorest* (least economically developed) countries have the *highest* percentage cost of per-capita GDP—*six-and one-half times* the cost of the richest countries! To gain a better perspective, please review the following data:

	No. of legal procedures required	No. of days needed	Entry cost as % of per capita GDP
U.S.A.	4	7	1%
Europe+Switzerland (avg.)	8.8	62	16%
Japan	11	50	11%
75-country (avg.)	10	63	34%
Rich countries (top 25%)	-	-	10%
Poor countries (bottom 25%)	-	-	65%
African countries	-	-	85%

The above data largely explain why less-developed countries (LDCs) tend to remain constantly in the economic doldrums. These data also point the way toward solving the persistent problems of long-term economic stagnation and high levels of unemployment that plague LDCs and which, in turn, generate poverty, poor health, and social unrest.

What is the answer? The answer is relatively easy to give, but would be a bitter pill for civil rulers to adopt, because doing so first requires a drastic change in a country's world-and-life view. People in positions of power and influence would find it necessary to voluntarily give up some of the existing political/social perks which artificially raise their own incomes far above the income of the average citizen. The workable solution is simply to make it easier and less costly for would-be entrepreneurs to do what they do best—that is, to freely serve the needs of other individuals in society in the hope of earning a profit. God has gifted many individuals in every society, and at all levels of the social structure, with a natural or learned ability to provide desired services to the public, at the entrepreneurs' own risk, with the hope and expectation of earning future profits.

The Entrepreneurial Spirit

This entrepreneurial spirit is what makes the wheels of economic progress go round and round in free societies, but it is an economic reality that has largely escaped the notice or interest of most government rulers the world over! The reason is two-fold:

First, the political/social elite in every country is accustomed to enjoying very high levels of income that are largely the result of the aforementioned political and social perks which favor the upper classes at the expense of the common citizens. Few civil leaders are sufficiently munificent and interested in the welfare of the common people that they would be willing to forego such benefits.

Second, and just as important, every civil government in existence is based on and operates on edicts which are enforced by the threat of legal punishment. Therefore, civil rulers tend to lean towards the idea of *mandating* this or that, but tend to be strangers to the concept of *voluntary* cooperation between sellers and buyers in the competitive marketplace. Thus, civil rulers generally do not put much trust in accomplishing good in society through the *non-coercive* practice of voluntary persuasion that is found in free market economies.

The persistent problem of widespread economic stagnation and poverty experienced by the people in less-developed countries is nothing more than the long-term economic result of the failure of civil rulers in LDCs to follow God's word as found in Deuteronomy 28 concerning national blessings (1-14) and national curses (15-68). Note an important point: The list of curses is much longer than the list of blessings!

The World Is Governed by God's Law of Cause-and-Effect

In short, to translate chapter 28 of Deuteronomy into economic terms, we come up with this spiritual/economic advice: If the civil rulers of LDCs *really* desire to foster beneficial economic progress for the good of their citizens, they must embrace God's higher moral law and apply it to their own country. The legal statutes, customs, and social institutions of their country must be changed so that powers wielded by civil rulers will be limited only to the proper biblical sphere and role that God has established for civil government. That is, the laws and whole social structure of every country must serve simply as guarantors of biblical law and order to foster peaceful economic exchange between free and self-responsible individuals. This is the ideal to strive for, rather than having a cumbersome political bureaucracy which allows civil rulers to grow fat in positions of power by feeding off of the common people through bribes and the selling of political favors. Moses phrased the issue succinctly when he stood before Pharaoh some 1400 years before Christ and cried, "Let my people go, that they may serve me!" (Ex. 8:1).

God put mankind in a world ruled by His law of cause-and-effect. If civil rulers will obey God's law and limit themselves (Ah, *that* is the problem!) to wield only those just political powers granted to them by God—that is, to simply protect the individual right of each person to stand as a self-responsible individual before God—by protecting each person's God-given right to engage in free economic production and exchange, then God will richly bless their country with peace and bountiful economic prosperity. This is the cause-and-effect promise of Deuteronomy 28. If God's law is embraced, rich economic blessings will follow; but if God's law is not embraced and put into practice, the long list of curses in Deuteronomy 28 cannot be avoided.

Many secular-minded economists fail to recognize that there is a *spiritual* basis to what is called "economic science." But, in truth, the sequence of economic cause and effect in God's created universe always moves from a *spiritually oriented cause* to an *economically expressed end*. In short, we find this sequence: Good morals produce an atmosphere of individual freedom coupled with self-responsibility which, in turn, produces rich economic blessings. Debased morals unerringly and ultimately produce the loss of people's individual freedom and self-responsibility before God which, ultimately and inescapably, produce social chaos and the many economic curses found in less-developed countries. This explains the crucial importance of moral leadership and limited civil government to the well-being and prosperity of every country in the world. Economically advanced countries ignore this inescapable cause-effect sequence at their peril. Alfred Edersheim, in writing about the evil rule of Athaliah, Queen of Judah, in the Old Testament writes:

> Indeed, this is one of the lessons which throughout make the history of Israel typical of that of the Church, and in a sense of all history, and which constitute its claim to the designation of "prophetic." In it events move, so to speak, in step with the utterances of the God of Israel. No direct or sudden interference seems necessary; but in the regular succession of events, each deviation from Divine order and rule, each attempt to compass results by departure from God's law and word, brings with it, not success, but failure and ruin.[2]

Since World War II our country has wasted multi-billions and billions of Americans' tax dollars (coercive levies that fall on ordinary people) through so-called "foreign aid" programs that have only served to enrichen favored political elites in foreign countries and to build tyrannical socialist regimes throughout the world. These same "foreign aid" programs have also subsidized certain large American international corporations which have excelled in "milking" their special-interest ties with U.S. political leaders. (Yes, our country also has many hidden special-interest elites who feed off the common people!) The long-term result has been the creation of unconstitutional bureaucratic governmental institutions such as the U.S. Export-Import Bank and its related entities, the World Bank, NAFTA, the WTO, and other socialist/fascist entities. All of these serve to destroy the God-given freedoms of the common people, both here and abroad. All of this is the direct result of the failure of civil rulers, not only in the LDCs but also here in America, to adhere to God's biblical law. In short, too many ungodly laws implemented by civil rulers actually run counter to God's higher law.

Economic systems don't develop in a vacuum. They are the cause-effect result of underlying spiritual forces which impact, first upon man's theological views, next upon man's philosophical views, then on his political views, which gives birth to the economic system. The sequence is shown in the diagram below:[3]

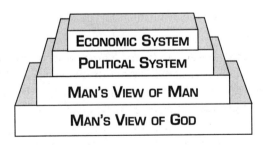

ECONOMIC SYSTEM
POLITICAL SYSTEM
MAN'S VIEW OF MAN
MAN'S VIEW OF GOD

John Eidsmoe, in the foreword to a new reprint of Thomas Cooley's 1880 book, *The General Principles of Constitutional Law of the USA*, issues a warning which both the people and political leaders of LDCs as well as America might well take to heart:

> If one were to say that State-worship is the official religion of the United States today, one would be guilty of exaggeration. But not by much.
>
> Increasingly, Americans today look to the state as the supreme authority, the ultimate lawgiver, the grantor of all rights and privileges, the cure for all ills, the solution to all problems, the source of all blessings, the guarantor of all security, even the arbiter of right and wrong. In return, the state increasingly demands of its citizens their absolute loyalty, their unquestioning obedience, and ever-growing portions of their wealth for sustenance.[4]

Read the above quote again! The mentality of America, once the "home of the free and the brave," is gradually becoming more and more like that of the godless civil rulers in LDCs. This is, at heart, a *spiritual* problem, and if it is not soon reversed, the effect in our country will eventually be the same! Unless we return to God's spiritual truth in America, we will suffer from the very same economic maladies that the LDCs suffer from. The line of cause-and-effect always works from the *spiritual* to the *economic*, not the other way around. The spreading of economic largess all over the world through coercive government mandates has never been the solution to economic poverty in the LDCs or at home, and it never will. The best help we can provide in eliminating poverty in less-developed countries is to serve as a shining beacon of a biblically based free-enterprise system at work. We must eliminate the wasteful and expensive practice of spreading tax-based American "foreign aid" all over the world. And we should, in the process, return the coercive tax-levies to the American people, to whom the money really belongs. Doing this will drastically reduce the spread of statist socialism throughout the world while, at the same time, reducing the ability of political elites in LDCs to manipulate and convert American "foreign aid" payments so they cannot continue living at the expense of their common people. Eliminating the "legal theft" of foreign aid will also bring to an end the long-term government subsidies to American corporations (a form of legalized theft through government decree). And ending these corporate subsidies would also serve to dissipate one of the major incentives that corporations have to lobby the Congress for continued special-interest handouts of tax dollars. As a result, the great and vastly expensive "Kublai Khan edifice" that has been built in Washington, D. C., through many years of special-interest lobbying, would receive a mortal blow, to the benefit of taxpayers throughout these United States of America. The true practice of biblical-based free enterprise here in America would then, by example, stimulate its acceptance by peoples all over the world.

Notes

1 Steve H. Hanke, "Slow Starters," Forbes (30 April 2001): 34.

2 Alfred Edersheim, Bible History, Old Testament, vol. 7, The History of Israel and Judah (n.p.:1876-1887; reprint, Grand Rapids: Eerdmans Publishing Co., 1980), 10 (page reference is to reprint edition).

3 Tom Rose, "Civil Government: A Distributor of Higher Law," chap. in Free Enterprise Economics (Mercer, PA: American Enterprise Publications, 1988), 7.

4 Thomas Cooley, The General Principles of Constitutional Law of the USA, with a Foreword by John Eidsmoe (n.p., 1880; reprint, Bridgewater, VA: American Foundation Publications, n.d.)

III
Money and the Federal Reserve

5

INFLATION—MADE UNDERSTANDABLE

Cease, my son, to hear the instruction that causeth
to err from the words of knowledge.
- Proverbs 19:27

Since the stock market crash of 1987 the official word issued
by both the Federal Reserve Board and our national government in Washington, D.C., is that there has been little or no
inflation.

Nothing could be further from the truth! In fact, the official statements about "inflation" by Federal Reserve Chairman
Alan Greenspan and the U.S. Department of Commerce are
simply part of a grandiose deception designed to mislead the
public so they won't think clearly. The reason for the grand
deception is that people who have trouble thinking clearly about
economic and monetary issues can be more easily manipulated and controlled. Manipulated by whom? and for whose
benefit? Manipulated by and for statist-minded presidential
administrations; by and for their hired bureaucrats; and by and
for globalist-minded special-interest entities who always stand
ready to sacrifice the welfare of their countrymen and their
own country for monetary gain. How true when the apostle
Paul warned that "the love of money is the root of all evil!" (I
Tim. 6:10).

Now, I realize that my words are harsh and that they smack of collusion and conspiracy in high places. Therefore, let us go back a bit in history.

The classical definition for inflation was very simple and straightforward. Economists once correctly defined inflation simply as an increase in the money supply. Understanding this easy-to-grasp definition, when people noted a persistent rise in the general level of prices they were able to readily perceive that a *prior* increase in currency and credit (money) was the underlying cause of the general rise in prices. And, even more importantly, they therefore knew what must be done to correct the problem: Civil rulers must be made to rein in their voracious tendency to spend more money than citizens were willing to pay in taxes; and private bankers had to reduce their creation of bank credit.

It is important to note that when banks extend loans to customers, the bankers actually *create* the money they lend to borrowers. The economic effect is exactly the same as if the bankers were counterfeiters who illicitly print the unearned money they spend! In short, when counterfeiters spend the money they print they inject new, unearned purchasing media into the economy. A similar increase of unearned purchasing media occurs when bankers lend printed bank notes or computer-generated checkbook credit to borrowers. Few bankers really understand that they are in the business of creating money!

Early Banking

Early banks were established on reserves of specie (gold and silver coins), but they also had legal authority granted to them to have their own unique bank notes printed for them by private engravers. The bank notes were thus nothing more than privately-issued "IOUs" (i.e., credit slips) which were only partially backed up by specie reserves held in each bank's vault. This partial-reserve system is called fractional-reserve banking, and it has hidden dangers.

Around 1850 the use of checkbook money in America grew to be as popular as bank notes. Thus people had their choice of credit when applying for a loan. They could opt for an issue of credit either in the form of newly printed bank notes or a newly written bank check. In either case, the extension of a loan to a customer by the bank resulted in an immediate injection of newly created money into the economy. This new increase of credit-money into the economy, relative to the fixed supply of existing goods and services, thus served to fuel a subsequent rise in the general price level. The monetary inflating process works exactly the same today as it did in the 1800s before the Federal Reserve Bank was created, and before modern computers were used to obfuscate the money-creation process. The modern process is just more sophisticated.

In short, monetary inflation occurs when banks extend loans (the supply of circulating money goes up); and monetary deflation occurs when borrowers repay loans (the supply of circulating money goes down). My point in explaining how early banks systematically created and destroyed money in their normal course of extending loans and later accepting repayments is this: The insidious process of monetary inflation and deflation used to be much easier for ordinary people to understand; but now with the existence of the Federal Reserve System and computer-generated credit, the entire process is much more difficult for people to understand. And what people do not understand, they are unable to control. For over three decades I would carefully share this maxim with students in my Money and Banking classes:

> The process of money and banking—of the creation and destruction of purchasing media—is very simple to understand. It just *appears* to be complicated and difficult to understand; and this is *not by chance!* For, man cannot control what he is unable to understand. Let me warn you that your economic and political freedom depend on your clear understanding of money and how it can be systematically created (monetary inflation) and destroyed (monetary deflation) by the banking system in collusion

with government-created central banks (like the Federal Reserve Bank).

Let me give a simple example: Picture me with a toy balloon in my hand. I put the balloon up to my lips and blow air into it. Result: the balloon expands. I have *inflated* the balloon! Assume that the air I expel from my lungs into the balloon is money, and assume that the circumference of the balloon represents the general price level. With each huff and puff more air (money) is injected into the balloon (the economy), and the result is that the circumference (the general price level) rises. This is what monetary inflation (injected air into the balloon) and subsequently rising prices (the growing circumference of the balloon) is all about. Note carefully that monetary injection occurs *first*, and prices rise as a *result*.

Confusion of the Language

The problem facing us today is that the clear language of yesteryear has been quietly changed. The former easy-to-understand thought process—that excessive money creation (i.e., inflation) *today* will subsequently lead to rising prices *tomorrow*—has been insidiously changed. And when new meaning is attributed to once easy-to-understand words, the people are easily confused; and with the confusion of words, there is an accompanying confusion of thought! Has this happened by chance? Not by a long shot!

Today, the federal government, the Federal Reserve Bank, every major financial publication, the controlled news media, and the vast majority of textbooks *all* refer to inflation as a general rise in prices. Why and how did the change occur from a *correct* and *easily understood* definition of inflation—an increase in the money supply—to one that is *incorrect*? Is it a question of widespread *planned collusion and deception*? Or is it simply a matter of stating, "That's just the way it happened. It was simply the result of a chance occurrence!"

Different observers will come up with differing opinions and explanations. But a pertinent saying comes to mind: "Follow the money!" People with similar interests are naturally drawn together, like birds of a feather that flock together. My answer to the above question is this: The *correct* definition of inflation leads people naturally to think from the *cause* (injection of newly-created money) to the *result* (a subsequent rise in price levels); while the *incorrect* definition of inflation (a rise in the general price level) leaves people to wonder what the underlying *cause* is! In short, the confusion of terminology leads to confused thinking and hiding of the truth. A quick review of some historical points will help shed some light.

Historical Background

During the Great Depression of the 1930s John Maynard Keynes came up with a novel idea for solving the problem of widespread high unemployment. His idea was especially enticing to civil rulers in Great Britain and these United States of America. It was this: Keynes claimed that the high level of unemployment could be solved if civil governments would expand their spending, not through increased tax levels, but rather by *creating* additional purchasing media (monetary inflation) and then spending it on various government "make work" projects. He argued that a general rise in price levels would *not* occur because the economy was suffering from deflation. He further argued that a general rise in price levels would not occur unless the civil authorities carelessly inflated the economy beyond what he called the "full-employment level."

Keynes' idea of government spending without increasing taxes was just too attractive for politicians and their hired bureaucrats to pass up. The Roosevelt Administration anxiously took the bait and got immersed in the longest and worst depression in our history. It was really the massive World War II deficit spending that finally revived the U.S. economy; but continued deficit spending by the federal government, and the resultant expansion of credit through the Federal Reserve Bank and the banking system (monetary inflation), largely explain the long lasting post-World War II inflationary spiral of wages and prices which have continued up to the present time. The inflationary spiral is an inevitable part of what is called "fine tuning the economy."

Today we are propagandized by the Federal Reserve Board that rising wage levels and/or rising prices for gasoline at service stations will *cause* inflation. Frankly, this is gobbledygook! It is a grossly false statement that is purposely designed to *mislead* people in their thinking! How can rising prices (a result) be the *cause* of rising prices? The plain answer is that rising prices *cannot* cause a general rise in the price level unless it is accompanied with even *greater* injections of new money and credit into the economy. Remember my example of blowing air into the balloon! Rising wages do *not* cause inflation; nor do higher prices at gasoline pumps cause inflation. Rather, wages paid to workers and gasoline prices at the pump are simply market prices. Like all other market prices, they simply reflect the *prior* injections of new money into the economy.

These new monetary injections are brought about by quiet collusion between various special-interest groups:

1) the federal government, which aggrandizes its political and economic power over citizens by continually engaging in deficit spending;

2) the Federal Reserve Bank, which is the inflationary vehicle used by the federal government to monetize the IOUs (bonds) that are created through deficit spending;

3) the banking system, which relies on the Federal Reserve as an inflationary "lender of last resort;" and

4) various large corporate business and labor union interests who are early recipients of the newly created money.

All of these entities, except the labor unions, have a special interest in shifting the blame of continually rising price levels onto workers, who are only interested in preserving the purchasing power of the money they receive in wages. But labor union leaders and certain corporate leaders have been in the forefront of encouraging civil authorities to follow inflationary policies. In matter of fact, Keynes' idea of fostering government spending through deficit spending rather than through increased levels of taxation was a sick scheme designed specifically to fool workingmen into accepting lower "real wages" while rising price levels quietly undermined the purchasing power of workers' paychecks.

Government leaders, some labor union leaders, and big business firms in Britain accepted Keynes' scheme as an insidious way of fooling labor union members into working for lower wages. They mistakenly thought that workingmen would be too ignorant to recognize the fact that their paychecks dwindled in purchasing power as the government, the central bank, and the banking industry quietly, but steadily, inflated the money supply.

The idea was for industrial leaders and government leaders to acquiesce to union members' militant demands for higher wages, but then to purposely erode the purchasing power of their higher wages by inflating the money supply through government deficit spending. This was the unsavory economic scheme that was so readily adopted, first by the government and business leaders in Britain, and then also by the Roosevelt Administration when Keynes paid a visit and explained his scheme to FDR in 1935. The result has been a 70-year wage-price spiral in these United States of America, from before World War II to the present. This explains why the purchasing power of a dollar in 1940 is now worth less than eight cents! Actually, if we look at the value of the dollar before the establishment of the Federal Reserve System, which began operation in 1914, we find that the 1913 dollar has been so depreciated in real purchasing power that it is now worth about two cents. That is about a 98% loss in value!

In short, the point I am making is that, since the establishment of the Federal Reserve System in 1913, a *planned collusion* of long-term monetary inflation has quietly bilked Americans of multi-billions of dollars of their hard-earned savings. This has especially served to impoverish elderly people who rely mainly on fixed-income retirement money from insurance and pensions. And this same inflation that has produced the long-term wage-price spiral has made it increasingly necessary for mothers to leave the home and enter the work force. In addition, this same monetary inflation has encouraged once-freedom-minded Americans, not only to acquiesce in, but even to seek various socialist/fascist government programs that have quietly eroded our historic economic and political freedoms.

Lost Riches, Lost Freedom

Americans would be much, much richer today if this planned deception of monetary inflation had not occurred. We would also be enjoying much, much greater political and economic freedom too, which is even more important than the lost economic riches. This systematic long-term monetary inflation and the resulting long-term wage-price spiral simply could *not* have happened without the *knowing acquiescence and collusion* of leaders in civil government, the Federal Reserve, private banks, big business, and big labor unions. To claim otherwise is to suggest that such leaders are ignorant of the working of economic cause and effect; and these entities are anything but ignorant!

Many people have been led to believe that an increase in wages is the cause of higher prices in the marketplace. But one thing I can assure you of is this: The wages people receive in the marketplace are *not* the cause of what today is wrongly called "inflation" (i.e., rising prices); but rising wage levels are, rather, the later *effect* of prior monetary inflation surreptitiously brought about by the conniving of the special-interest groups mentioned above. A wage is nothing more than a specific price that, like all prices, respond to monetary inflation.

Since the market crash of 1987, the Federal Reserve Bank— in cooperation (perhaps collusion would be a better word to use!) with past and current presidential administrations and hidden special-interest groups—has freely pumped multi-billions of new money annually into both our domestic and the world economy. And with the recent potential threat of bank runs induced by fear of Y2K (which did not occur), the Federal Reserve pumped additional billions into the banking system, which it is now attempting to offset without inducing another deflationary spiral as the Federal Reserve did cause in 1929-39 and again in 1973-74.

Question: Why has the massive monetary inflation engineered since 1987 failed to generate correspondingly high rises in the general price level? To make a complicated answer short, *it did*! But, the impact of the money creation has been somewhat softened and diverted. Let me explain:

First, economic observers are increasingly making the claim that government statistics do *not* accurately reflect the true level of rising prices. Any homemaker can readily substantiate this claim. Statistics can easily be "groomed" by excluding some prices and giving different weights to others.

Next, civil governments and central bankers *can create and inject as much money* as they wish into the economy, but they *cannot control <u>where</u> the money goes* once it is injected. Over the last decade or so *trillions* of dollars have been created. Domestically, much newly-created money has been funneled into the stock market. Thus, we now have the greatest credit bubble in history! Lately, it has shown signs of bursting. It is impossible to predict when or how the inflationary bubble might burst and when the feared downturn in the stock market and in economic activity might occur.

Another part of the diversionary aspect of engaging in monetary inflation is that recent presidential administrations, the Federal Reserve Bank and various foreign central banks, and international banks and businesses have worked hand-in-hand (collusion?) to decapitalize much of America's basic industry—even to the point of shipping entire manufacturing plants overseas. The result of this collusion (much of it accomplished at taxpayers' expense) has been to generate an artificial industrial boom in less-developed countries with low wages (especially Red China, who regards America as her primary enemy). As a consequence, a great influx of cheaply-made, shoddy goods has put many American workers out of work. This is why we have not seen rising prices for certain consumer goods which must compete with foreign imports. This helps explain why the officially promulgated statistics don't show the full expected effects of the monetary inflation that has been taking place since at least 1987.

A Lesson to Learn

Is there a lesson to be learned? Yes! There is a double-sided lesson to be learned:

First, a freedom-loving people must carefully guard their common vocabulary so that the historic meaning of words will not be insidiously changed. Failure to take this precaution will lead to a certain confusion of terms and thence to confused thinking by the general populace.

Secondly, a freedom-loving people must constantly ponder the following question regarding civil government and keep the answer foremost in their mind: *What is the proper role of civil government in society*? Is its proper role to manipulate and control the business cycle in an attempt to foster economic security for citizens? Or is its proper role simply to maintain law and order with the goal of maximizing each individual's freedom and self-responsibility before God?

The biblical answer to this question is very clear, but it won't be readily accepted by the majority of Americans because they have been spoon-fed the unbiblical idea that the proper role of civil government is to attempt to ensure their economic security with the hope of full employment, rather than simply allowing people to stand free and responsible before their Creator. "It's the economy, Stupid!" has become the cry, and its acceptance by a populace unfamiliar with economic history will lead to certain enslavement.

This truth is so important that it bears repeating: There is one all-important question that freedom-minded Americans should be asking: "What is the proper role of civil government in society?" How Americans answer this question will determine whether they are to live, as self-responsible individuals in a peaceful environment of God-given freedom, or (as they are living today) under an inherently brutal regime of government-imposed fascism, not only at the national level, but ultimately on a global scale.

The preservation of God-given freedom requires a people who can think clearly and be guided by biblically oriented principles. A true understanding of what monetary inflation really is, and the subsequent price effects produced by government-induced monetary inflation, will certainly equip people to think more clearly. But to do so, we must protect the integrity of our vocabulary. Be on your guard, your hope for freedom demands it!

6

ALL ABOUT GOLD

"All About Gold" first appeared in early 1972 as a series of essays in a syndicated newspaper column entitled *Tom's Corner* by Tom Rose, professor economics and money and banking. At that time it was still illegal for American citizens to own gold coins and gold bullion. President Franklin D. Roosevelt had issued an Executive Order in 1933 which dictatorially deprived citizens of their historic right to own gold. They were forced, under penalty of "law," to turn in their gold to the U.S. Treasury in exchange for government-created fiat paper money.

From 1933 onward the federal government regulated the price of gold at $35 per ounce. Years of worldwide government monetary inflation followed, and the purchasing value of the U.S. dollar, as well as the value of other nations' currencies, plummeted. As a result, an unsustainable "two-tier" price for gold developed—one was the "official government" price, while the other represented a true free-market price which reflected the vast increases of fiat money that governments had pumped into world markets over the years.

Over the next three decades succeeding presidential administrations and the U.S. Congress have continued massive deficit spending, and as a result, the purchasing power of the U.S. dollar has continued to decline.

One step remains to restore lost economic freedom and citizen control over the political process to citizens. What is that step? It is to match citizens' right to own gold with a return to a gold-coin standard. This updated chapter explains how gold ownership coupled with the legal right to redeem government-created fiat money for gold is essential for protecting and preserving man's freedom and self-responsibility before God.

> With thy wisdom and with thine understanding thou
> hast gotten thee riches, and hast gotten gold
> and silver into thy treasures:
> - Ezekiel 28:4

F our generations of Americans have grown up in almost complete ignorance of gold. They neither appreciate gold as the precious and valuable metal it is, nor do they understand or appreciate gold's indispensable role in protecting man's economic and political freedom.

Because of the continuing unsettled conditions in the world's monetary markets, and since the overwhelming majority of schools do not convey critically needed information about gold to American youth, it appears timely to discuss the subject of gold and how it benefits mankind. And because of my special interest in the welfare of the ordinary family man who works for a living, I will try to show how the precious right to buy, own, and sell this valuable property helps him to protect his own interests. Though many people mistakenly regard gold only as a rich man's commodity, it is my sincere belief that the legal right to own gold and to have it as a basic monetary unit helps the hard-working family man, more than any other member of society, to safeguard his economic independence.

What is Gold?

First, *what is gold?*

It depends upon whom you ask. A chemist would explain that gold is a heavy metal that has an atomic weight of 197 and a density of 19.3 grams per cubic centimeter. Gold has a melting point of 1,063 degrees Centigrade, and it boils at 2,600 degrees Centigrade. Gold has been known to man since prehistoric times, and modern man has assigned an atomic number of 79 to it.

An economic historian, on the other hand, would give a completely different answer: Gold, he would explain, is a precious metal which men during all ages and in all parts of the world have valued more highly than any other metal. Because of its unique qualities, gold, since the early dawn of history, has served man both as a dependable medium of exchange and an invaluable storehouse of value.

During periods of political and social unrest which have plagued the world throughout history, men have tended to look with suspicion on the doubtful value of money minted or printed by civil rulers. But men have never lost faith in gold as a medium of exchange or as a storehouse of value. The poor man who has been prudent and foresighted enough to hoard a few gold coins in anticipation of the possible advent of evil days has consistently and invariably discovered that other people's insatiable desire for gold provides him the means of buying safe passage or food for his loved ones. The same truth holds, to a lesser extent, for silver.

Some people deride gold as a rich man's commodity. They think that the right to own gold benefits the rich man at the poor man's expense. But the lessons of history teach otherwise. Gold is man's great economic equalizer. The poor man who has gold can use it to bargain as an equal with the rich man. Gold has been a faithful servant throughout history to all who have relied on it in time of need: king, merchant, craftsman, laborer, farmer, tenant, or peasant. The man who has a few gold coins will have economic security in time of need because he has real bargaining power. The man who lacks gold in times of crises has always been forced to rely on the fragile mercy of his fellowmen, which often breaks under the stress of adversity.

The biblical scholar would substantiate the testimony of the economic historian in favor of gold, but he would add a still richer dimension. Gold, he would say, is the first metal to be mentioned in the Bible (Gen. 2:11). It is the only metal mentioned before the fall of man, and the mention is favorable: "And the gold of that land is good" (Gen. 2:12).

Gold is next mentioned in Genesis 13:2 where we are told that Abram became very rich in cattle, in silver, and in gold. This highly prized commodity is mentioned so often and so favorably in the Bible that the reader cannot help but gain a favorable impression of it. More than once the kings of Israel and of Judah used gold from the temple to buy military protection from surrounding kings. It is interesting to note that favorable mention of gold spans the entire Bible. Gold is mentioned in the second chapter of the first book of the Bible (Gen. 2) as well as the second last chapter of the last book (Rev. 21) where we are told that the Holy City and its streets will be paved with gold transparent as glass.

Why Does Gold Have Value?

Some proponents of gold become over-zealous and make the mistake of claiming that gold has intrinsic value. That is, they claim that gold has value in and of itself. This idea, of course, is erroneous, as modern economists and psychologists will agree. Nothing has inherent value. Value, like beauty, exists only in the eye of the beholder. You cannot feel, touch, or weigh value because it exists only in your mind. One man's prize is another man's burden.

Nothing can have intrinsic value because all value is imputed, that is, we mentally place a value *onto* an object. A person *imputes* value onto an article or a good because he forms an opinion about its potential desirability or usefulness. This is true whether we speak about the food we eat, the wood we burn, the paintings we enjoy, or the persons we love.

People prize gold for the utility derived from it. We have already seen that gold provides the man who has it with a sure means of securing food, shelter, and safety for his family in time of need because people everywhere regard gold as a unique storehouse of value and as a universally acceptable medium of exchange. It is these functions which provide gold's main economic value in society.

But individuals also value gold for reasons other than its utility in social relations. These reasons are not difficult to deduce. Gold is scarce. It is warmly beautiful. It is durable almost to the point of being indestructible. Gold never rusts or dissolves. It lasts almost indefinitely—long after other metals have become corroded or oxidized. Of the common acids, only a mixture of concentrated nitric and hydrochloric acids (aqua regia) will dissolve it. Even strong acids, when used alone, do not affect the chemical stability of gold. It always retains its beauty.

Gold is one of the most ductile and malleable metals known to man. It can be melted and shaped without harm. Gold can be hammered into exceedingly thin leaves—about twelve thousand to the inch. When alloyed with other metals—such as silver, which is its natural alloy in nature—gold improves in hardness while still retaining its beauty.

Finally, the natural scarcity of gold assures that it will always have a prominent place in the comparative scale of man's esteem. For some psychological reason, man seems to impute value to those things which are in scarce supply.

In short, if one believes in a providential and sovereign God (as this writer does), it would appear that gold is a unique and precious gift of our Almighty Creator to man. Let me ask: Could it be that God gave gold the very physical properties that would cause man to value it *because* He knows (predetermined) that such a commodity would be useful in preserving man's God-given freedom? Humanist skeptics who deny the existence of a Creator who purposively planned and sustains the universe moment-by-moment would, of course, scoff at such an idea as being unscientific. But such thoughts are not unscientific; they merely transcend the limited scope of science into the more important and basic fields of philosophy and theology.

The Spiritual Significance of Gold

A Christian might ask, "I'm a Christian, so my eyes are on heaven and not on earth. Why should I then be concerned about a grossly material thing like gold?"

To this question I would reply that, while gold *is* a material or worldly thing, it also has a *great spiritual significance* that many professed Christians have apparently overlooked. Let me explain: Christians believe in the doctrine of individual self-responsibility before God. That is what salvation by grace, justification by faith, and Christian good works as a result of God's saving grace are all about. Man is responsible before God, first for the choice he makes about Christ, and then, once saved, for everything he does thereafter. Saved sinners are called to be faithful *servants* of God; but this requires that they be *free* so that they can be responsible for self to God.

But self-responsibility presupposes the *inward* freedom to choose and the *outward* freedom to act upon one's choices. Without freedom of choice man cannot be self-responsible. Many libertarians recognize this truth. But there is a deeper spiritual aspect of this truth to consider: The *mental act of choosing* (an internal process) demands an *outside economic guarantee* of that action. This is where the role of gold comes into play. Without the economic freedom to validate his choices, man cannot be truly free; he cannot truly be a responsible trustee to God for the wealth he holds during his stay on this earth. Read the Parable of the Talents (Matt. 25:14-30). In short, how can man be morally responsible for the disposition of his goods and the application of his spiritual gifts unless he has economic control over them? The spiritual significance of gold is that it helps guarantee the outward material base that man needs, by his God-given nature, to be spiritually free and self-responsible on the *inside*; that is, to be a self-responsible being created in the very image and likeness of his Maker.

Why Don't Governments Want Citizens to Own Gold?

The crucially important role of gold in preserving man's freedom from energetic civil rulers is not understood at all in this age of mushrooming government bureaucracy. People today have come to regard civil government as a father-protector and supplier of their daily needs—a role which the Bible says belongs to God alone. Modern man has forgotten the most obvious lesson of history: More often than not, civil governments have enslaved their own citizens under the guise of "caring for them." Some examples from ancient history are Egypt, Greece, and Rome. Examples from the Mercantile Age are Spain, France, and England. And some modern examples under the world-wide thrust of socialism are Italy (Mussolini), Germany (Hitler), Russia (Lenin and followers), England (Fabian Socialists), and finally these United States under our unique brand of state-welfarism.

A look at history reveals that rulers eventually strive with citizens over the "power of the purse." The important issue that citizens through the ages have had to face has been: *Who* is to have power over spending the incomes that free citizens produce through their creative economic activity? Is it to be the *rulers?* Or is it to the *people* themselves?

Rulers have always answered this question by imposing taxes to the maximum that citizens will endure before rebelling. And just before this point has been reached, civil rulers have generally turned to debauching the currency. In olden times kings clipped gold and silver coins or melted them down to recast them with a mixture of baser metals. The debased coins, by fiat of the king, were then to be accepted by citizens at their old face value. This led to hoarding of the older, more valuable coins and the passing on of the newer, debauched currency and to recognition of "Gresham's Law."

In the thirteenth century Marco Polo returned from China and reported in glowing terms how the great Kublai Khan financed an extensive program of public works and public welfare by forcing citizens to surrender their gold and silver in exchange for paper currency made out of the inner bark of mulberry trees. Had Marco Polo remained in China a few years longer he would have observed the economic and social chaos that followed such monetary debauchery.

What's the point? Simply this: We learn from history that rulers have tended to enslave those whom they are committed to protect by forcibly relieving citizens of their rightful freedom to spend their own money as they wish. When citizens will no longer peacefully bear heavier tax burdens, rulers turn to the insidious method of stealing purchasing power from citizens by inflating the money supply. Each new unit of money created by the ruler, just like money manufactured by illegal counterfeiters, competes in the open marketplace on an equal par with the money already held by citizens. Thus, wealth is stealthily but surely transferred from the private hands of citizens to the collective control of government bureaucrats. And the faster the ruler creates more new money, the faster additional wealth is transferred to him from the control of private hands. Private wealth thus becomes socialized through debauchment of the currency. Citizens thereby lose economic control over their own destinies.

This insidious debauching of the U.S. dollar has occurred on a grandiose scale in these United States of America. For instance, in 1932—the year before Americans were denied the right to convert their government money into gold by presidential order—our national debt was only $19.4 billion ($156 per person). But by 1970, only 38 years later, the national debt had soared to a monstrous $384 billion ($1,875 per person). And by the year 2002 the "admitted" debt was almost $6 trillion while the *real* debt is a *multiple* of that amount! Every indication is that even larger increases in our national debt are coming in the future. Each succeeding president, with a pliant Congress, saddles the American public with billions of dollars of additional debt.

Economic Seduction Leads to Political Slavery

This constantly rising government debt has been incurred through a highly sophisticated process of debauching the currency. This method is used today by all government-sponsored central banks throughout the world. It is also used by the Federal Reserve Bank. Every new dollar of this mounting debt represents a new dollar of purchasing power that bureaucratic rulers have quietly and insidiously siphoned away, through credit manipulation and monetary creation, from the control of private citizens. As this process of siphoning away the purchasing power of people's money continues, an ever-growing number of once-free-and-independent citizens is seduced into looking for their sustenance from the very bureaucrats who insidiously steal from them. The end result of such monetary seduction is political and economic slavery.

I have given here the historical background of *why* civil rulers do not want citizens to have the right to own gold and especially for citizens *not* to have the ability of legally forcing the government to pay out gold in exchange for government fiat paper money. In summary, rulers do not want people to be free to convert government-decreed money into gold because the right to do so provides a haven of safety and economic independence for frugal wage earners. The right to convert government-created money into gold provides a strong bulwark against both political and economic enslavement. And this is a freedom that statist-minded politicians and government bureaucrats *do not* want citizens to have.

When ordinary citizens have the legal right to take government money to their local bank and demand gold for it, they, in effect, have only the same option that any poker player has when the stakes get too high for his comfort—the option of "cashing in his chips" and sitting out on the sidelines for a while. By cashing in their government-decreed money-chips for gold, citizens can indirectly, but surely, "veto" the grandiose spending plans of government lawmakers and bureaucrats. But rulers—because they want *to* control, rather than *be* controlled—find it exceedingly distasteful to allow this kind of economic veto power over their actions to reside in the hands of ordinary citizens.

Can Gold Protect?

"But," a person might ask, "can the right to own gold help citizens protect themselves from the tendency of rulers to enslave them?"

My answer: There are two kinds of control that citizens *must* maintain over political rulers if they hope to preserve a republican form of self-government. First, and most obvious, is *political control*. Citizens must have the power to replace elected officials whenever they become dissatisfied with their performance. Political control is assured by requiring elected representatives to stand for reelection at regular intervals. The powers of impeachment and recall also help to preserve at least a semblance of citizens' political control between elections.

But there is a *second* kind of control which is less obvious but just as important for effective control by citizens over civil rulers. This is *economic control*. It is only natural for politicians to try to escape from the economic control exerted upon them by the citizens who provide tax monies for their support. Control over others, after all, is what the deadly game of politics is all about. And political power rests on economic power. So, if citizens are to have any hope of remaining independent from power-hungry individuals who from time-to-time find their way into office, they *must* preserve their "economic veto" over politicians and government bureaucrats. Economically *independent* citizens are able to control their political servants, but economically *dependent* citizens are destined to fall under the control of politicians and their hired bureaucrats.

Gold Provides Citizens with "Veto Power"

Without this day-to-day "veto power," it is only a matter of time until citizens surely lose effective political power over the politicians they elect. When citizens lack this power, politicians find it relatively easy to seduce citizens with their own tax money. Demagogic office holders do this by inflating the money supply and then "buying" the votes of unthinking citizens by spending the newly-created money on vote-getting projects. It has become almost impossible today to unseat an incumbent president who wants to be reelected because he has billions of dollars of "stolen" (newly created) inflation dollars under his control.

This is exactly where the crucial role of gold comes into play: When a country is on a gold standard, the amount of money in circulation is tied to the amount of gold held in reserve by the government treasury or the government-created central bank. When the government's gold reserve rises, the money supply can be correspondingly inflated through the banking system. Prices will subsequently tend to rise as a result. When the amount of gold held on reserve falls, the opposite happens. The money supply will be correspondingly restricted, and prices will fall.

How does the right to own gold give citizens economic power over politicians under a gold standard? In this way: When politicians engage in deficit spending they must either *borrow* the money they want to spend, or they must *create* it by inflating the money supply. Since it is easier and less noticed by citizens to inflate than to borrow, politicians usually choose to inflate. To the extent that they do this, they legally rob citizens by stealth of their hard-earned wealth.

Gold Allows Citizens to Act Individually

But when some of the more astute citizens become aware of this robbery by stealth, they become worried and start cashing their government-decreed money-chips (Federal Reserve notes) at banks and ask for gold in exchange. And, as banks pay out gold they are forced to replenish their dwindling gold stock by withdrawing gold from the government treasury. This, in turn, causes what gold reserve is left in the treasury to be inadequate to sustain the existing money supply. Banks are then forced to call in loans and thereby gradually restrict the money supply until it again comes into balance with the smaller gold reserve held by the central bank or the treasury.

This is the way efforts of politicians to inflate through deficit spending can be effectively counteracted under a gold standard by the independent and straight-forward actions of private citizens. The ensuing loss of public confidence in government leadership serves to force the politicians to cancel their plans for further deficit spending. Thus, the *economic power* wielded by a growing number of concerned citizens serves to maintain their *political power* over government officials. But when this crucial economic power is absent—as it is today and has been since 1933—politicians are free to spend, spend, and spend until they are able to enslave the populace. Since 1933 American citizens can no longer surrender their government paper money in exchange for gold. This explains how gold-backed money serves as the protector of man's freedom. The 1933 restriction against citizens' right to own gold was removed in 1973, so we now have the right to personally own gold; but the *convertibility* of Federal Reserve Notes back into gold has *never* been restored. This fact largely explains America's present flight into totalitarianism. The continued loss of convertibility makes it impossible for American citizens to impose a monetary "veto power" on government spending. This condemns citizens irrevocably into the hands of the central bank money manipulators who collude with politicians to insidiously steal the citizens' accumulated wealth.

Goodbye Gold Standard!

Why did the United States go off the gold standard?

In order to understand *why* the United States went off the gold standard in 1933, we must understand the series of events which produced the pressures that made this crucial step possible. We must go back almost twenty years earlier and trace step-by-step the growing influence of the federal government in our economy.

First, the background:

1913—Congress voted to create the Federal Reserve System, allegedly to provide the business community with an "elastic" currency. The alleged idea was to prevent financial panics like the one that occurred in 1907, which some economic historians attribute to the business uncertainty fostered by the "trust busting" vendetta of President Theodore Roosevelt.

In arguing against the bill which would create the Federal Reserve System, Senator Elihu Root (NY) warned,

> . . . It does not provide an elastic currency. It provides an expansive currency, but not an elastic one. It provides a currency which may be increased, always increased, but not a currency for which the bill contains any provision compelling reduction.[1]

1914-1917—During the early part of World War I, England and France purchased war material from U.S. business firms on a cash basis. When their foreign exchange credits were used up, our federal government authorized continued selling to the Allies on credit. Much of the political pressure for selling on credit came from those business and labor interests that had an economic stake in the continued export of war material that they produced. The needed credit was created and sustained by government borrowing and by monetary inflation engineered through the newly formed Federal Reserve System.

1917-1918—Continued financial and material support of the Allies by the United States produced a growing strain with Germany which culminated in open warfare. A total of about two-thirds of the cost of World War I was financed by borrowing and by monetary inflation through the Federal Reserve System.

It is very doubtful that the American people could have been led into war in the absence of the government's ability to finance the war through monetary inflation brought about by the Federal Reserve Bank. The lesson is obvious: A people who prefer peace to war should never arm their civil rulers with a central bank because it provides the government with power to engage in monetary inflation as a means of financing war-induced debt!

1919-1930—Our inflated money supply caused prices to be higher than they otherwise would have been after the war. This produced two effects: First, a tendency for imports to rise, which was opposed by business firms, farmers, and labor unions who faced growing foreign competition. This economic problem was handled politically by passing a series of higher tariff laws:

1921—The Emergency Tariff Act, which placed higher duties on wool, sugar, wheat, and other commodities.

1922—The Fordney-McCumber Act, which established the highest tariff rates up to that time. This Act gave the President power to raise or lower tariff rates at his discretion. President Coolidge raised rates several times.

1929—The Smoot-Hawley Tariff Act was introduced before the Crash, in April of 1929. During the Presidential campaign of 1928, Herbert Hoover had campaigned in favor of a higher tariff.

The net result of this series of protective tariffs was a decline in foreign trade—foreigners could not *buy from* us unless they were able to accumulate credits by *selling to* us.

This led to the second effect: In order to finance sales to foreigners, in the absence of allowing foreign goods to enter the United States, huge amounts of foreign loans and bonds were floated in our country by bankers and financial underwriters. This constituted a *privately*-financed type of "foreign aid" similar to the post-World War II *publicly*-financed foreign aid program. When Americans reduced their "investments " in these foreign bonds and notes in mid-1928, exports soon declined substantially. From the end of World War I to 1929, over nine billion dollars were lent overseas in an effort to shore up our sagging export markets.

Some Loose Threads

Now we must backtrack to pick up some other threads:

1923—This was the year that Federal Reserve officials accidentally stumbled upon an interesting fact: They discovered that their *purchases* of government bonds in the open securities market tended to stimulate short-run business activity by inflating the money supply. From this point on the Federal Reserve started pursuing a *planned* policy of attempting to *manipulate* the level of business activity through what is now called Open Market Operations. In short, the United States moved another step towards the socialist/fascist ideal of a *planned economy* with this new discovery of manipulative money power.

1924-1927—A series of manipulative efforts by Federal Reserve authorities produced a generally "easy money" policy:

1924—The Federal Reserve increased the money supply to help Britain reestablish a quasi-gold standard. She had abandoned the gold standard during World War I.

1927—The Federal Reserve again followed an "easy money" policy to help sustain British and other European currencies and to stimulate the sale of American commodities abroad.

1928—By this time it was clearly evident that much of the new money that was being created through the Federal Reserve and the banking system was finding its way into speculative activities: Both real estate prices in Florida and stock market prices in New York were soaring.

Federal Reserve System = Engine of Inflation

Federal Reserve officials belatedly found out that they could *inflate,* but that they could not control *where* the new money might be spent. Thus we see an evident truth: It was the misguided policy established by Federal officials—and *not* private speculators—that was the root cause of the inflationary boom which preceded the 1929 Crash. *Few people realize this important fact.* Another fact that is not widely recognized is this: When monetary contractions occur in this age of monetary manipulation, the contractions are usually initiated by the central banking authorities. And the unsophisticated public—the "small" investor who has slender financial reserves—is the one who gets hurt. When banks call in loans, there is a net flow of wealth from the public to high-placed professional money managers.

1929—By mid-year Federal Reserve officials decided upon a deflationary step in order to dampen the rampant speculation that their "easy money" policy had produced. The Federal Reserve raised the discount rate to a high level. This forced banks to liquidate loans and thereby produced a sharp contraction in the money supply. The sharp drop in stock prices that started in October, 1929, was induced by this sudden deflation of the money supply, triggered by the Federal Reserve.

1929-1933—During the next four years the Federal Reserve followed a deflationary policy by perversely collecting on loans from financially shaky banks. These banks, in turn, put pressures on their own customers, who were forced to liquidate their investments, even if it meant selling at a loss. By mid-1932 the money supply had dropped by 30-percent, and our country was in the depths of the Great Depression.

Stage Set for "Reflation"

The stage was now set to abandon the gold standard in an effort to "reflate" the economy. And this 1930s type of "reflation" through monetary manipulation has continued long-term with only a few interruptions ever since.

I do not mean to imply that the post-World War I economic intervention, the misguided attempt to "correct" the resulting economic maladjustments through monetary inflation, the sudden deflation, the financial crash of 1929, and the ensuing depression of the 1930s were *purposely* planned or masterminded by some evil force that was consciously intent on getting these United States off the gold standard. (Such a conspiracy-view of history is, of course, certainly within the realm of possibility, and some historians hold this view.) My personal view is that this is the chain of events which just naturally occurs when fallible man attempts to play God by intervening in the natural working of the competitive free market process.

The Culprit Plays Hero

First, the 1929 Crash and the ensuing depression were the *direct result* of earlier massive monetary and economic interventions by the federal government.

Second, when bad trouble finally came, the culprit attempted to play hero by engaging in even grosser interventions of the economy: The economic dislocations produced by earlier federal mismanagement were *wrongly* blamed on businessmen and free enterprise *as a system.* The terrible economic maladjustments that occurred *as a result* of federal mismanagement were thus used as excuses for *further* federal interventions and controls which have continued and grown ever-more stringent up to the present time.

It is doubtful whether the *degree* of federal intervention that we have today could ever have been imposed on American citizens without first going off the gold standard and thereby denying citizens their historic right to redeem government-created dollars for gold. This, as I see it, is *why* the gold standard was *intentionally* abandoned by U.S. political leaders: *Elimination of the gold standard served to make citizens more dependent eco-nomically and thereby more responsive to political manipulation by federal politicians and bureaucrats.*

How did these United States go off the gold standard?

The step-by-step process by which U.S. political leaders eliminated the gold standard provides a classical study of *planned duplicity*.

First, the background: Our country was in the very depths of its most severe depression. The severity of the depression had been brought about by the economic and political meddling of two persons—one a President, and the other a President-elect.

In a vain attempt to reflate the economy after the 1929 Crash, President Herbert Hoover called industrial leaders to Washington and asked them to hold wages up, even in the face of falling prices. Many leading industrialists, to their later sorrow, cooperated. Those who did cooperate caused serious harm to the financial stability of the firms they headed. This served to reduce employment in the long run and thus lengthened the downward trend of the economy. It practically guaranteed a Democratic victory in the 1932 election because voters tend to blame the incumbent Administration for existing woes.

The election of Franklin D. Roosevelt served to produce deeper economic and political instability because he refused to cooperate with the outgoing Administration. From November, 1932 (when he won the election), until March, 1933, (when he was officially inaugurated), Roosevelt refused to make any policy statements to alleviate the growing sense of alarm of the financial and business community. Roosevelt was interested only in making partisan political gains by thoroughly discrediting the Hoover Administration. And the *worse* things got before the inauguration, the *better* chance Roosevelt had of personally looking good when he came into power.

1933: The Fateful Year

Now we come to the historical record of what happened when Franklin D. Roosevelt took office as President:

March 6, 1933—Roosevelt, as one of his first official acts, closed all banks by Executive Order and forbade them to pay out specie (gold) in exchange for paper dollars.

March 10, 1933—Four days later Roosevelt prohibited, again by Executive Order, the export of gold without a license from the Treasury Department. By removing free export he effectively removed the U.S. from the full gold-coin monetary standard we had been on since 1879 (except for the wartime emergency between 1917-1919).

April, 1933—A month later Roosevelt issued another Executive Order which nationalized the gold of citizens at the existing official price of $20.67 per ounce. Under penalty of law American citizens were forced to exchange their gold for government-created paper dollars. On April 19 he stopped the free movement of gold. This gave formal recognition that these United States had departed from the gold standard.

These actions were taken because Professor George F. Warren of Cornell University had convinced the Administration that any attempt to reflate the economy would stimulate an *outward* flow of gold from the banking system, from the U.S. Treasury, and from the country unless the government imposed an embargo on it. Warren realized that a free people would invoke their "veto power" on political leaders by turning in their untrustworthy paper government money for gold, which they trusted. So, once American citizens were legally "locked in" from obtaining gold, the politicians were free to engage in deficit spending to their heart's content. Citizens then no longer had any way of stopping them short of political revolt.

June 5, 1933—Congress, at the Administration's request, passed a joint resolution which voided any and all gold clauses in public and private debts.

October 25, 1933—President Roosevelt authorized the Reconstruction Finance Corporation to buy gold at prices to be determined by himself and the Secretary of the Treasury, Henry Morgenthau. They set the price at $31.36 per ounce to start—a price near the free world price—and gradually raised it over the next few months to $35.

January 30, 1934—Congress passed the Gold Reserve Act. This formalized President Roosevelt's earlier actions of nationalizing gold *without* legislative sanction and gave him legal power to devalue the dollar by raising the price of gold.

January 31, 1934—The next day Roosevelt issued another Executive Order. This one officially devalued the dollar by 41 percent by raising the price of gold to $35 per ounce. (Note: The price of gold was raised only *after* citizens had been forcibly relieved of their gold at the *lower* price of $20.67.)

This act officially confirmed and completed the nationalization of citizens' gold. It had the ultimate effect of placing these United States on a fiat (paper) monetary standard domestically. Monetary control over U.S. politicians and their hired bureaucrats was thus effectively and legally wrested from the hands of citizens. Now federal officials would be free to manipulate and reflate the economy as they wished without having to worry about the threat of adverse reactions by economically independent citizens. The way was now cleared for a more complete government-controlled economy. The door was now opened to the easy financing of future wars: World War II, the Korean War, the Vietnam War, the war in Kosovo, the Mid-east Gulf War of 1991, the current "War Against Terrorism" (2001) in Afghanistan and other Mid-east countries, as well as the many "peace keeping" activities our country now engages in so regularly all over the world. In short, monetary inflation to finance government debt fosters "perpetual war" in seeking the elusive goal of "perpetual peace."

Is Gold Impractical Today?

People sometimes ask, "Isn't it impractical to think that these United States can ever return to the gold standard? It seems that there isn't enough gold in the world to sustain the expanded volume of trade. Wouldn't a return to the gold standard throw us into another depression?"

These questions are based on two erroneous assumptions about gold that have been deliberately promoted by those who oppose the right of citizens to own gold and/or to have the legal right of redemption of paper money for gold:

First, gold is *not* used to *sustain* trade between nations. Rather, it is used to compensate for *imbalances* in trade. For example, the total annual trade between these United States and foreign nations might be as low as $.5 billion or as high as $50 billion or more. As long as exports and imports are in balance between each country, no gold will be exchanged. The only time a country gains or loses gold is when a *sustained imbalance* in trade occurs. Thus, there is no limit to the *total volume* of international trade that can be sustained by the official gold reserves held by central banks throughout the world. The problem isn't the *amount* of gold in existence, but rather the problem is to keep the prices of both goods and currencies *flexible* so that trade will stay in balance.

Much nonsense about gold has been promulgated by political leaders, economists, and others who should know better. The "shortage of gold" myth is just one of the nonsensical claims made by those who make a fetish of deriding gold as a "useless and outdated trinket."

Question: Why should so many otherwise knowledgeable experts so consistently and so volubly deride such an obviously useful metal as gold???

If gold *is* so useless, why did the *entire* world output of gold in 1971 (40½ million fine ounces, worth about $1.4 billion at $35 per ounce) disappear into private hands? Someone, many someones, obviously didn't trust their own governments to hold that gold output for them! If gold is so useless and worthless, why do governments and central banks want it concentrated in *their* hands?

People's historically wise distrust of civil governments and their preference to hold gold instead of government-created paper money during times of political and economic uncertainty testify, not to their foolishness, but to their good sense! The long history of money teaches that civil governments are counterfeiters at heart and, therefore, cannot be trusted with the dangerous power to control money. If America's founding fathers made one mistake, it was certainly their decision to give the United States Congress power to regulate the value of money. The original intent of the founders has been twisted to go beyond fixing the gold and silver content of minted coins into an excuse for establishing a central bank which is capable of manipulating economic activity as well as stealing the value of citizens' hard-earned savings.

The second erroneous assumption of the above questions can be shown by an interesting incident from American history: The Union had abandoned the gold standard during the War Between the States because political leaders chose to finance the war through borrowing and through inflation of the money supply instead of by imposing higher taxes on citizens. (This bloodiest war of American history would certainly have been avoided without the federal government being able to finance the invasion of the South by borrowing and creating money.) "Pay-as-you-go" plans for financing wars make citizens much more reluctant to go to war. Monetary inflation, as usual, produced rising prices. After the war a "hard money" administration decided to return to a sound currency by reinstituting gold redemption (i.e., by paying out gold specie to citizens who wanted to buy gold with paper dollars). Many wild statements had been made which predicted imminent disaster if gold payment were reinstituted. But what really happened?

An Historical Example

When these United States reinstituted gold payments on January 2, 1879, gold started flowing *into* the country and *into* the Treasury because people regained faith in the honesty of the government of our country. Shortly after, the so-called gold-resumption business boom got underway. Thus ended the longest period of business contraction in United States history. Yearly imports of gold looked like this:

	Imports	Exports
1879	$ 5.6 million	$ 4.6 million
1880	80.8 million	3.6 million
1881	100.0 million	2.6 million

Why shouldn't a return to sound money with the right of gold redemption today produce the same beneficial results as it did in the 1870s?

Here is how it could be done:

The price of gold has been artificially controlled and/or manipulated for so long by the federal government and the Federal Reserve Bank in collusion with other central banks of the world that no one has an accurate idea of what gold is truly worth today. We *know* it would be higher! During the early 1970s the price of gold soared to over $100 per ounce in the world market when the U.S. no longer artificially held the price down to $35. During the early 1980s the price of gold soared to $850 per ounce. And today the price has dropped to less than $300 per ounce. The price of gold is presently near a 20-year low. But this price does not represent a true free-market price because the government-created central banks of the world have been colluding with each other to hold down the price of gold. Why? Because the price of gold is widely regarded as an "inflation indicator," thus, if the price of gold is seen to be low, then it is assumed that there has been no monetary inflation because consumer and commodity prices have not risen.

In short, to explain why governments attempt to manipulate the price of gold: Political leaders today are attempting to hold the price of gold down to hide their untrustworthiness as protectors of the purchasing power of their currencies. Rising prices (and consumer and commodity prices *will* start rising in the near future) would reveal the inflationary monetary policies they have been following!

Franklin D. Roosevelt's totalitarian act in 1933 of unconstitutionally confiscating the gold of American citizens through his Executive Order is now no longer in effect. In 1973 Congress passed legislation which restored the right of Americans to own gold. That was a good step because any citizen can now take his or her government-created "poker chips" (i.e., the Federal Reserve Notes we call "dollars") and purchase gold coins or gold bullion at whatever government-manipulated "market" price that happens to exist. But something *very important* is still missing! When Susy Smith buys gold today she simply buys it from some John Doe who receives her dollars in return. Her buying of gold has *no impact at all* on the inflated money supply that has been created through the Federal Reserve Bank's financing of federal government deficits. In short, neither the Susy Smiths nor the John Does of America have any economic "veto power" over the deficit-spending plans of our politicians and bureaucrats in Washington, DC.

Needed: A Return to a Gold-Coin Standard

What is needed to restore the lost economic freedom and lost political power of American citizens is to return to the gold-coin standard that Roosevelt robbed us of with his illegal Executive Order in 1933. A return to the gold-coin standard would accomplish these important things:

• American citizens would once again regain control over their elected officials by having an independent economic "veto power" over politicians' spending plans. By simply deciding to take government-created money to the bank and demanding payment in gold, any citizen can gain the economic safety of holding gold while simultaneously helping to overrule politicians' tendencies to engage in inflationary deficit spending.

• The persistent decline in purchasing power of the U.S. dollar can be halted. For instance, the purchasing power of a dollar saved in 1940 is now worth less than eight cents! But under a gold-coin standard a dollar saved today would tend to retain its full purchasing power for many years into the future.

• The level of taxation and the intrusion of the federal government in the lives of American citizens would rapidly decrease.

• A new spirit of freedom would sweep over our country and *real* economic growth would soar upward.

• American citizens would once again control the people they elect to office rather than being controlled by them.

This simple process is all that is needed to put these United States back on a sound-money basis. It would help to reestablish people's waning confidence in our federal government. Such a step not only makes good sense economically, but it also makes good sense politically when viewed from the people's welfare. It would restore to citizens the important economic control over politicians and government bureaucrats which they lost under the Roosevelt Administration in 1933 when our country abandoned the gold standard.

Who Will Control Whom?

Will enough liberty-loving citizens see the wisdom of how a return to a gold-coin standard can help them regain control over their own civil government—not only for their *own* benefit, but for the benefit of their sons and daughters? My head and experience warn me that the American public is likely to remain too apathetic to demand that our federal government restore the precious right it raped from them 70 years ago. But my heart keeps hoping!

Let us remember that the right to own gold coupled with a restoration of the gold-coin standard provides those who hold gold with economic independence and power. The question to be answered is: *Who is to control whom?* Will the *people* control the agency of civil government which they set up to keep law and order? Or will they be controlled *by* the agency of their own creation?

Let us not forget that money under a gold standard retains its integrity, while fiat money (paper money that cannot be redeemed) does not because civil government then has no restraint against inflating the money supply—thus insidiously robbing the very citizens who created civil government.

Today gold is loudly and uniformly denigrated by most of our political leaders, so-called financial experts, and statist-minded economists. And the price of gold is wallowing near its 20-year low. This is occurring while the Federal Reserve has been publicly mouthing a "conservative" monetary policy, even while it has, in actuality, been stoking the fires of monetary policy to induce worldwide inflation. This has served to create a wonderful buying opportunity for brave and observant individuals who are not fearful of going against widespread public opinion.

Recent and continuing Federal Reserve monetary policy, and the monetary policy of other countries too, practically guarantee future rises in the price of gold, the commodity which is God's provision to protect the economic and political freedom of the ordinary man.

Finally, let us remember the old French proverb, "We have gold because we can't trust government." Also, let us not forget that nothing is better for the preservation of a republic than a healthy suspicion of civil government by economically independent citizens!

Notes:

1. *Congressional Record*, 63d Cong., 2d sess., vol. 51, pt. 1 (13 December 1913), p. 831, a & b. Also found in Tom Rose, Economics: The American Economy from a Christian Perspective (Mercer, PA: American Enterprise Publications, 1985), 219.

7

NINE STEPS FROM FULL-BODIED
MONEY TO FIAT MONEY

And the gold of that land is good:. . .
Genesis 2:12

1. The people freely come to use, through voluntary choice and common acceptance, full-bodied gold and silver coins as a generally acceptable medium of exchange. No government mandate or control is needed for this; it is a natural development in a free society. Thus, we see that the appearance of money in society is a natural development of the unregulated free-market process.

2. The civil authority *declares* by legal fiat that the people's prior choice is "legal tender;" that is, the people by law are *forced* to accept in payment of debts what they have previously been willing to accept all along. The legal fiat has no practical effect immediately, for the civil authority simply ratifies by law what the people are already doing, but it *will* have a very practical impact later.

3. The civil authority issues *representative* money (gold or silver certificates) which it promises to redeem upon demand by guaranteeing to hold a specified amount of precious metal on reserve. Government authorities find they must do this in order to maintain the confidence of the people.

The representative money is also declared to be "legal tender."

4. The desire of civil rulers to expand government spending in excess of tax revenues soon occurs, so additional amounts of "representative" money are periodically issued. This "representative" money is really *fiduciary* money because it is issued in excess of the amount of precious metal held on reserve for redemption. At this point all of the money issued by the civil rulers *cannot* be redeemed for precious metals, for no longer is there enough precious metal held in reserve to make full redemption. The people do not yet suspect that their money is being insidiously and intentionally debauched by the monetary authorities, so they remain unconcerned.

5. Finally, such vast amounts of representative money (really fiduciary money) are issued that certain observant individuals become worried, and they start turning in their paper money for redemption. Government officials honor requests for redemption for a time, but they soon realize, as more and more people redeem their gold and silver certificates in exchange for real gold and silver, that it will be impossible to long continue honoring the government's promise to redeem all the paper money that has been issued in excess of the reserves held. The cruel fact is that the vast majority of the supposedly "representative" money is not really represented by real money held on reserve. The people's money has been knowingly and insidiously debauched by the very government the people once trusted. Thus, the promise of convertibility to precious metal is ultimately officially repudiated. Since the money has previously been officially declared as "legal tender," most people still are not too disturbed. For, though prices have been climbing, the people mistakenly believe by now that the government's act of declaring money as "legal tender" somehow gives it an intrinsic value. And, since the people generally *continue* to blindly *accept* the money in exchange for goods and services, the money, in an economic sense, *is* still money.

6. The people's money is now nothing more than *fiat* paper money. It is fiat money even though it still *looks* the same as the money the people have gotten used to, first as *representative* money, and then as *fiduciary* money. The ever-increasing flood of fiat money continues as the government is more and more pressed, by political pressure, to increase spending beyond tax revenues. Prices, which had gradually begun creeping upward after each increase in the money supply, now begin to spiral higher and higher.

7. Finally, a hyper-monetary inflation occurs. The quantity of fiat money is eventually expanded so rapidly that it loses practically all of its purchasing power. Too many pieces of paper money are chasing the limited supply of goods and services; this causes prices to soar upwards. (The German inflation of 1921-23 is an excellent example.)

8. The people finally start refusing to accept the debauched currency. They begin, by common choice and general acceptance, to let something *else* play the role of money. Thus, some new commodity that is generally accepted by the people *becomes* money — it becomes money because it is *willingly* accepted as a medium of exchange by the people – and the government paper fiat money thereby *ceases* to function economically as money. The new commodity may be a precious metal, chocolate candy, cigarettes, etc. The only necessary requirement is that the people be generally willing to accept it in exchange for goods and services. And this occurs *in spite of* any action taken by the ruling authorities. Finally, the people usually turn once again to gold or silver as a common medium of exchange because of the inherent characteristics given to these metals by God at the creation of the earth. Order thus begins to grow out of chaos — chaos that was caused by the government's debauching of the original currency in the first place.

9. But the government authorities now step in (as in Step 2) and once again declare the people's new money to be

"legal tender" by legal fiat. Thus the whole monetary debauching process begins anew.

Practically every civil government in the history of mankind has (or is currently) engaged in the above described process of monetary debauchery. Why? Because governments tend to be the world's greatest "legal counterfeiters." They ultimately conspire to get more and more money to spend—that is, more money than the people are willing to pay directly in taxes. Consequently, there is always an ever-growing incentive for civil rulers to insidiously (stealthily and quietly) appropriate a larger portion of the people's wealth by intentionally, but secretly, debauching the currency. The control of real wealth is thus easily transferred from the control of citizens to civil rulers as continued monetary inflation quietly generates rising price levels. The last thing a freedom-loving people ever want to do is to entrust the money-making power to their civil rulers. Thousands of years of history have proven that civil rulers are the greatest "legal" counterfeiters the world has ever known. Peasants all over the world are known to prefer real gold and silver coins to the untrustworthy paper money issued by civil governments. This preference is well stated in an old French proverb, "We have gold because we don't trust government."

Civil rulers invariably break two simple but crucial rules of sound money:

Rule 1: Money must be *earned* before it is spent. Government-created money, like illegal counterfeit money, does not and cannot represent values which have already been produced and offered for sale in the marketplace. When civil rulers or fractional-reserve bankers create new money, the newly created money does *not* represent true earning power. Rather, the newly created money simply *dilutes* the earning power of previously existing money. This, of course, constitutes a moral wrong—a breaking of the commandment "Thou shalt not steal" (Ex. 20:15).

Rule 2: There must be a *balance* between the amount of money in existence and the quantity of goods and services that money represents. When government authorities or central banks continuously expand the money supply, people will react to the increased supply of purchasing media by taking the excess money and using it to buy goods and services in the marketplace or in the stock market, thus causing prices to rise. It is this upward spiral of prices which is popularly, but erroneously, called "inflation." But true inflation is actually the creation of new money by governmental authorities or the fractional-reserve banking system. The general rise in price levels is simply the *subsequent response* of the prior monetary inflation that has *already* occurred.

Let us hope that some day trusting Americans will indeed learn the one great and inescapable monetary lesson of history mentioned above: That civil rulers cannot safely be entrusted with the care of money, because they will always debauch it. The care of money can be safely entrusted only to private entities in a truly competitive marketplace under a 100%-reserve banking system.

IV

Governmental Interposition

8

THE ECONOMICS OF CIVIL GOVERNMENT

The kings of the earth set themselves,
and the rulers take counsel together,
against the Lord, and against his anointed,
saying, Let us break their bands asunder,
and cast away their cords from us.
- Psalm 2:2-3

As we begin our earthly journey into a new century, it is important to look over the last 100 years to see if we can learn anything about the social institution we call civil government. James Jackson, in volume 7, *History of the American Nation*, refers to an earlier age in which,

> An American may through a long life, never be reminded of the federal government, except when he votes at presidential and congressional elections.[1]

How things have changed! Today, Americans cannot escape the ever-present rules and regulations that emanate mainly from Washington, D.C., but also from our state capitols and local city halls. These political edicts besiege and attack us every hour of every day, as well as in every nook and cranny of our personal and business lives:

• We cannot escape FDA-mandated "Truth in Labeling" requirements at the breakfast table, in the medicine cabinet, or at the supermarket.

• Ninety-percent of American school children are enrolled in tax-supported government schools where parents have no effective input about either policy or curriculum content. It is in these same tax-supported schools where millions of young children are regularly prescribed government-approved mind-altering drugs which predispose young people to commit acts of violence when they approach puberty. These violent acts, in turn, provide government leaders with fodder for removing people's right to own and bear arms.

• Employers are minutely regulated regarding whom they can hire or fire. They also must provide working conditions, wages, and benefits mandated by government regulations. Finally, business firms are used by federal, state, and local civil governments as non-paid tax-collection agents by requiring them to make payroll deductions.

• Then there are even federal regulations which regulate how much water we are allowed per flush in our toilets! So much for the concept of structured federalism that was originally designed by our founding fathers!

How Did We Get Where We Are?

How did we come to lose the system of widely dispersed and carefully limited political powers that were intentionally designed by our founding fathers, only to end up today with citizens being suffocated by a centralized fascistic government which voraciously eats up the economic substance of the people? For, until the very early 1900s—in spite of Lincoln's calculated destruction of the Constitution and the unconstitutional Reconstruction Acts after the War Between the States—the average American continued to enjoy a high degree of economic freedom.

The strong arm of the federal government, as James Jackson indicated above, did not yet touch the ordinary citizen in his daily activities. Fascistic regulation of business at the national level began with the Interstate Commerce Act in 1887, which established the Interstate Commerce Commission (ICC). The ICC grew out of a U.S. Supreme Court decision—*Wabash, St. Louis and Pacific Railroad Company v Illinois* (118 U.S. 557) 1886. This decision served to deny states the power of regulating interstate commerce and gave it to the federal government.

After 1900 bureaucratic intervention by the federal government in the lives of citizens gradually increased. Here is a selection of federal agencies with dates of establishment: Food and Drug Administration, which grew out of the Food and Drug Act (1906); the Federal Bureau of Investigation, which resulted from a presidential "executive order" (1908); The Federal Reserve Bank (1913); the Federal Trade Commission (1915); the Federal Power Commission (1920); the Federal Deposit Insurance Corporation (1933); the Federal Communications Commission (1934); and the Federal Housing Administration (1933). The intent of our founding fathers under the Articles of Confederation was that the power of the central government would *not* be able to touch citizens directly. The above listing shows how their intent has been systematically undermined, thus culminating in the powerful centralized government we have today.

To answer the question of how we lost our original system of widely dispersed governmental powers and devolved into a centralized system of freedom-smothering fascism is this: The American people fell into the same trap that the Old Testament Israelites fell into when they asked for "a king to judge us like all the nations" (I Sam. 8:5). In short, they looked to the civil authority to provide what God said *He* would provide—their economic sustenance. What started out as a moderate level of government intervention in citizens' business and personal lives in the early 1900s gradually accelerated into an ever-increasing army of government bureaucrats to regulate and tax. Each succeeding generation of Americans has been mentally conditioned to look more and more to the civil authority for their economic sustenance. This occurred in spite of our Lord's clear instructions that we are to ask our Father in heaven, "Give us this day our daily bread" (Matt. 6:11). We are *not* to make that supplication to our civil rulers, which would be idolatry! The sad result of our spiritual rebellion has been a steady increase in both governmental regulation and oppressive tax levels: In 1900 no American citizen was directly taxed by the federal government; and less than five-percent of his income was taxed away by civil government at *all* levels—local, state, and national. Today the Congress has power to tax at any rate that is politically acceptable to brain-washed citizens.

Today, *all* citizens are unconstitutionally subject to the never-properly-ratified Sixteenth Amendment (the Personal Income Tax). But only a relatively few members of the political elite—and certain millions of low-income citizens, many living in subsidized housing and receiving various government subsidies—can effectively escape the major brunt of the personal income tax. And low-income groups are carefully maintained and crassly manipulated by political power brokers to guarantee that there will always be an ignorant, but self-interested, "cheering section" to avidly support the constant drive for increasing government expenditures. Thus, the effective control of citizens' wealth and income is insidiously transferred from private hands to a powerful controlling fascistic government elite.

Economic Analysis

Let us analyze the working of civil government so we can understand it, for what man does not understand he cannot control. Then we will make biblical applications to provide a godly orientation to undergird our understanding; for good theology leads to wholesome political rule which, in turn, produces a beneficial economic climate in which free-market exchange can take place for the benefit of everyone. Let us remember an old French proverb: "Civil government is a watchdog to be fed, not a cow to be milked!"

First, we must recognize that the institution of civil government is *coercive* by its very nature. Civil rulers act by *mandating*, and they *punish* those who refuse to acquiesce to their mandates. I have often advised students, "It is absolutely impossible for the civil authority to perform a charitable act. Its very God-given nature is to use force. 'Do this, or else!' is always its threat." Sometimes a student would state, "But, sir, I pay my taxes voluntarily!" My reply was always, "But what would happen if you 'voluntarily' decided *not* to pay your taxes?"

Recognizing the inherent coercive nature of civil government leads us to these questions: Since civil government is, by its very nature, a *coercive* agency of society, is there any *limit* to the level of taxation that morally can be imposed on citizens? Also, are there any restrictions as to *what* tax monies should be used for?

From an economic viewpoint we find that when tax levels start exceeding 15- to 20-percent of people's income or 15- to 20-percent on the price of goods and services, people start seeking ways to avoid paying taxes. Thus, black markets spontaneously appear. From a biblical viewpoint, we see that God requires only one-tenth (a tithe) of our incomes. When the civil authority starts mandating as much or *more* than ten-percent of a person's income, does not the civil authority place itself equal to or higher than God? Only a "theologically challenged" citizenry (to coin a new "politically *incorrect*" term) would succumb to such tyranny instead of rising up in open rebellion!

In short, then, the answers to the above questions are:

• Yes, there *is* a moral limit that a free and godly people should place on the taxing power of civil rulers. When the personal income tax was unconstitutionally placed on citizens in 1913 (remember that it was not properly ratified), the vast majority of citizens were *exempt* from paying taxes, else they would never have permitted such a privacy-invading tax. The top tax rate was six-percent on incomes in excess of $500,000, which would be equivalent to almost $9 million today! The general populace would never have endured a personal income tax, except that they were seduced to do so under the illusion that the tax would always be plundered from the privileged wealthy class while their own incomes would remain exempt from taxation!

• Yes, there are both *moral* and *constitutional* restrictions as to what tax monies should be used for. The Constitution of these United States of America limits the federal government to using tax monies only for "the common Defence and general Welfare . . . ." But, during the administration of Franklin D. Roosevelt in the 1930s, the concept of "general welfare" was stretched unconstitutionally to finance a myriad of socialist schemes designed to redistribute the private wealth of citizens and to impose fascistic economic controls on business firms. FDR was a great admirer of Mussolini's fascist state in Italy, and he strived to emulate him in America. Succeeding presidential administrations—Lyndon Johnson's "War on Poverty," for instance—continued to fund and expand massive government-sponsored schemes of "legalized theft," which are euphemistically called "transfer payments." Since World War II, tax monies have been increasingly distributed, not only domestically, but also internationally to hundreds of nations in the form of "foreign aid." This serves as an unending cornucopia for special-interest groups that are closely tied to domestic and foreign civil governments. It also serves to foster the spread of socialist/fascist regimes in foreign nations.

Our Sinful World

We live in a world peopled by billions of sinful people who are alienated from God. These people—that's you and I!—are always ready to capture the reins of governmental power with an eye to lining their own pockets at the expense of others. The result is always some form of government-sponsored monopoly or other form of legalized favoritism, such as government licensing of professions and businesses. For an historical example, consider the English East India Company which was formed in 1599 and chartered by Queen Elizabeth in 1600. Its grant of monopoly power greatly enriched the privileged few. A more modern instance can be seen in government licensing of certain professions (attorneys, medical doctors, dentists, various building trades, etc.). The goal is always tight control over the number of new entrants into a profession. The economic result is always fewer practitioners who thereby earn much higher incomes financed by lower-income people. Government licensing is a superbly effective, but vicious, practice.

It lines the pockets of the privileged groups that are licensed, and their higher incomes are paid mostly by people with much lower incomes.

Our story of the symbiotic relationship between the political sphere and the economic sphere, and of how political power is used to suppress voluntary economic exchange in the competitive free market, could go on and on. But readers would quickly become weary of reading such a sad tale.

What Are We to Do?

Let us ask: Did God have an ideal model of economic exchange in mind when He created man, recognizing that God predestined man to live in a sinful world? I believe the answer to this question is a resounding YES! God instituted the social agency of civil government simply to maintain law and order so men could be free and self-responsible in their service to Him, their Creator (Gen.1:26-28; Ex. 8:1; Deut. 17:14-20; Rom. 13:1-4; I Tim. 2:1-20).

If the civil authority were strictly limited to the high ideal of applying only a *negative* force of punishing those who harm or plunder others, then godly freedom and self-responsibility among mankind would be maximized. Such a policy would unerringly lead toward an unending spiral of economic progress, personal prosperity, and world peace. Let us pray for this kind of reformation in civil government, which can come about only through our own personal reformation to God's word and His rule in our heart.

Notes:

1 Linda Bowles, "Government Has Mangled the Constitution," Conservative Chronicle, 24 November 1999, 19.

9

REBUILDING THE CRUMBLING FOUNDATIONS: THE BIBLICAL AND CONSTITUTIONAL RESPONSE TO GROWING TYRANNY

The following is an address delivered by Professor Rose at a symposium entitled "God's Law & Socio-political Reform" at Covenant Christian Church, Alleghenyville, PA, March 28, 1998.

> . . . fall down and worship the golden image that
> Nebuchadnezzar the king hath set up: . . .
> . . . be it known unto thee, O king, that we will not serve thy
> gods, nor worship the golden image which thou hast set up.
> - Daniel 3: 5 & 18

Recently my wife Ruth and I made a late-night stop at our local supermarket. As we were leaving with our purchases someone came up behind me and tapped me on the shoulder. I turned and looked up at a tall young man, immediately recognizing him as a former student. "Professor Rose, my name is Mike Wise. I studied economics under you a number of years ago. Do you remember?"

Of course I *did* remember Mike! He was a good student with an enquiring mind who did not hesitate to pose questions or to challenge me to defend what I said when it didn't fit with his presuppositions.

"You know," he said, "when I first heard what you had to say in Economics #101, I thought you were coming off the wall! But now not a day goes by without my seeing that the things you were saying are true!"

When I asked Mike what kind of work he is involved in, he replied that he is serving as a representative in the Ohio State Legislature from the Cleveland area.

Now, I mention this happy reunion for a purpose. Because today, like a few years ago with my-then student Mike, some of the things I have to relate might be a little disturbing. You also might think that I'm "coming off the wall." But if you will keep an open mind and take time to reflect on what I have to say—as disturbing as it may be—I believe that you will see that I have your own welfare and that of our country at heart, and that my warning and suggestions make sense.

A Warning and an Hypothesis

Let me start first by sounding a warning, and then presenting an hypothesis for you to consider.

First the warning: The people of America are much closer to losing their Republic than they realize. In fact, if positive steps are not *soon* taken to peacefully rebuild our Constitutional foundations and restore the historic fabric of our American Republic, it will be too late! I realize these are alarming words to share with such an erudite group as we have here today; but, sadly, they are true, as I will soon show you.

Now for the hypothesis that I suggest you consider. The information I am about to present, that is, the current socio/political/economic status of our country—the problems we face, and the solutions I will propose—are all based on a simple and straightforward hypothesis, which is: I believe it is possible, as well as instructive, to gain an insight of the moral fiber or quality of a nation (i.e., of the people of a country) by observing and measuring the trend and degree of the growth of centralized political/economic power in a country.

To state my proposition somewhat differently: A biblically oriented people will conduct their personal and public affairs in such a way that they will be blessed by God with a decentralized political/economic system, while a society who are strangers to, or antagonistic to, biblical principles will, contrariwise, be cursed by being enslaved by tyrannical rulers. Historically, these United States of America are a good example of the former, while Red China and the former USSR are good examples of the latter. (For a biblical citation: See Deut. 28:1-14 for a list of God's blessings to be bestowed on an obedient people and Deut. 28:15-68 for a list of God's curses on a rebellious people.)

Question: Did God have a reason to make His list of curses upon those who stray from His law much longer and more terrible than His list of blessings upon those who faithfully adhere to God's law-word? Could this have something to do with fallen man's inherent nature to seek enslavement and death rather than liberty and life? If so, O America, we have strong reason to be fearful and to tremble!

Examples of Tyranny in America

What are some examples of growing tyranny in America?

First, we need a working definition of tyranny. By tyranny I mean any form of oppressive power[1] exerted over man— that is, over man himself or over his property. Let us note that man's property, broadly defined, includes man's God-given freedom and ability to hold his own opinions, to act upon those opinions in his own self-interest and of his family. In short, man has a property right to conduct his affairs without interference from other entities in society—even from the various levels of civil authority, as long as his actions do not unjustly harm another person or another person's property.[2] The assumption which underlies all this, of course, is that we are always to be guided by the parameters of biblical principles in both our private and public lives.

I have often written about the growing threat of tyranny in these United States of America and the fact—for indeed it is a fact—that we are about to lose our constitutional form of government and that we are ripe to be "melded" into a tyrannical form of one-world humanistic government. Therefore, let me raise a patriotic cry of warning: High-placed leaders in our country are *right now* pursuing long-held secret plans to undermine and destroy the inherent, God-given freedoms which our founding fathers so carefully set up in our Declaration of Independence, the Constitution of 1781 (The Articles of Confederation, which was agreed to by Congress on November 5, 1777), the Constitution of 1787 (our present Constitution), and other founding documents like the Northwest Ordinance of 1787. Recent presidential administrations have undermined our constitutional rights. Both Democratic and Republican administrations have worked insidiously to hand our country over to the godless United Nations. One accomplishment I hope to achieve today is to help awaken a sleeping populace to this impending danger which threatens us, our children, and our grandchildren.

The Arrogation of Power Through Executive Orders

President Abraham Lincoln was the first president to use an Executive Order as a means of gaining unconstitutional power. In doing so he destroyed the U.S. Constitution under the guise of "saving" the Union. He issued Executive Order #1 on April 21, 1861, to call forth 75,000 militia to invade the Southern States that had legally seceded from the Union. Lincoln did this while Congress was not in session. Since he had no constitutional authority to issue such an Executive Order, he did so under the "authority" of martial law which he imposed. The U.S. Constitution gives only Congress the power to declare war and to raise armies, but Congress subsequently endorsed his action. (Most of the opposing votes in Congress, of course, had already left with the seceded States.)

Succeeding presidents of these United States followed Lincoln's lead in issuing Executive Orders, but mostly only for the internal governing of the Executive Department of the federal government. Between Lincoln and Franklin D. Roosevelt fewer than 2,000 Executive Orders were issued; but from FDR to the present, more than 17,000 have been issued.[3]

This brings us to a crucial turning point in America's history. Congress passed the "Trading With the Enemy Act" in 1917 during World War I.[4] This act defined "enemy" as foreigners and countries who were at war with these United States. It specifically *excluded* American citizens as enemies with these words ". . . other than citizens of the United States, wherever resident or wherever doing business, . . . "[5]

It is important to recognize that this Act was not terminated after World War I, but that it remained in force like a ticking time bomb ready to go off.

When Franklin D. Roosevelt was inaugurated on March 4, 1933, Congress was not yet in session. In his inaugural address Roosevelt said:

> I am prepared under my constitutional duty to recommend the measures that a stricken nation in the midst of a stricken world may require.
>
> These measures, or such other measures as the Congress may build out of its experience and wisdom, I shall seek, within my constitutional authority, to bring to speedy adoption.
>
> But in the event that the Congress shall fail to take one of these two courses, and in the event that the national emergency is still critical, I shall not evade the clear course of duty that will then confront me.
>
> I shall ask the Congress for the one remaining instrument to meet the *crisis—broad executive power to wage a war against the emergency as great as the power that would be given me if we were in fact invaded by a foreign foe.* (Italics added)
>
> . . . The people of the United States have not failed. In their need they have registered a mandate that they want direct, vigorous action.
>
> *They have asked for discipline and direction under leadership.* They have made me the present instrument of their wishes. In the spirit of the gift I take it.[6] (Italics added)

The very next day, March 5th, Roosevelt issued a proclamation calling Congress to a special session to start on March

9, 1933. On March 6th Roosevelt issued a proclamation declaring a "Bank Holiday" from March 6 to March 9, 1933. He had no constitutional authority to do this. Three days later, on March 9, 1933, Congress was presented with a bill "to provide relief in the existing national emergency in banking, and *for other purposes*" (Italics added). A compliant Congress was pressured to pass this bill *without congressional members even having had time to read the bill!*

This resulting act of Congress amended the "Trading With the Enemy Act" of 1917 so that it would apply to *American citizens* instead of foreign enemies! It reads:

> During time of war or during any other period of national emergency declared by the President, the President may, through any agency that he may designate, or otherwise, investigate, regulate, or prohibit, under such rules and regulations as he may prescribe, by means of licenses or otherwise, any transactions in foreign exchange, transfers of credit between or payments by banking institutions as defined by the President, and export, hoarding, melting, or earmarking of gold or silver coin or bullion or currency, *by any person within the United States or any place subject to the jurisdiction thereof;* . . .'[7] (Italics added)

In summary, a compliant Congress was very hurriedly pressured into passing into law, a bill which had been quietly and carefully prepared by the Roosevelt administration *before* Congress was ever in session. The resulting act extended to American citizens the controls that the 1917 Act had imposed only on America's enemies! It gave open-ended, dictatorial power to President Roosevelt to declare a national emergency *at his sole discretion* and then to act in any way he saw fit to solve whatever "national crisis" he seemed capable of conjuring in his mind. The President used this congressionally-bestowed power to arrogate unconstitutional powers to the Executive Department, which severely disrupted the previous balance of power between the Legislative, the Executive, and the Judicial Departments of our federal government.

Now comes the especially threatening aspect of this "War Powers Act," from a constitutional standpoint: This so-called "temporary" Emergency War Powers Act, which was carried forward in 1933 from World War I in 1917, is *still in force!* It has never been rescinded by any subsequent Congress, so *any* President *at any time, and for any reason,* can *still* declare a national emergency and instantly declare martial law that will throw American citizens under *a totalitarian dictatorship!* This situation is, in itself, a *true* national emergency of the greatest proportion! It threatens the very existence of our American Republic!

Collusion Between Our Political Leaders and the United Nations

◆ Department of State Publication 7277:

In September, 1961, the U.S. Department of State published a nineteen-page pamphlet entitled *FREEDOM FROM WAR, The United States Program for General Disarmament and Complete Disarmament in a Peaceful World.*

This document outlined a three-step program under which our country would be unilaterally disarmed while, at the same time, the military power of the United Nations would be gradually increased until no nation on earth, including our own country, would have enough military capability to withstand the power of the United Nations. In short, the plan was to establish the United Nations, a godless, morally and politically corrupt organization as a one-world dictatorship which would answer to no higher power, not even to God.

I first became aware of *Document 7277* in 1962. I ordered multiple copies from the Government Printing Office for distribution as a means of awakening a sleeping and unsuspecting populace of what our political leaders were doing. I would order more copies as I needed them. At that time they were priced at 15 cents each. In late 1962 the Government Printing Office returned my order stating "Out of Print." Over the years I continued to warn my students and others about the impending danger.

Even though *Document 7277* is still officially "out of print," the *plan* is still in effect. Right now American servicemen are serving in many foreign countries under the banner of the United Nations, and an estimate of between 400,000 and 800,000 foreign troops are stationed here in these United States of America.[8] We might ask ourselves "why?" Over 200 years ago American patriots went to war because King George III stationed foreign troops on American soil and tried to disarm American citizens. Our forefathers recognized the clear danger that armed foreign troops presented at that time, but today an increasingly disarmed citizenry seem to be strangely complacent about this serious threat to American freedom!

◆ Treaties Between the UN and These United States of America:

During recent years our country has become ensnared in various treaties with the UN. These treaties threaten the constitutionally protected rights of Americans. They do so by thrusting us under the authority of the UN World Court, by exposing Americans to international environmental "agreements," by handing over to UN control various parcels of American real estate through so-called "World Heritage Sites" and "Biosphere Reserves,"[9] as well as by a planned UN tax on U.S. citizens! Another plan that is insidiously being worked on is to disarm American citizens by having our Second Amendment rights taken away through UN treaties with various countries designed to disarm citizens all over the world. Citizens in Canada and Australia have recently been disarmed. Why should political leaders be so intent on disarming their own citizens? I don't have time to go into detail today on these items, but will be happy to point enquiring minds to sources of documentation.

◆ Government Control Agencies:

Many Americans are gradually waking up to the threat that such militant government agencies such as the BATF, DEA, FBI,

IRS, FEMA and others pose to their safety. The first three agencies are becoming increasingly notorious for their violent "swat team" tactics; and, indeed, they are to be feared! A complacent citizenry has, up to now, tolerated such unconstitutional shows of force on fellow citizens because the federal government has mentally and psychologically conditioned them to believe that such tactics are needed to "protect" us from drug runners, etc. But our own CIA, another federal agency, has been accused (correctly so) of flying tons and tons of illegal drugs into our country as a means of generating "off budget" operating funds.[10] The Mena, Arkansas, airport during the governorship of now-President Clinton was a notorious landing spot for such illicit trade. Videos and literature abound on this subject.

You know, income-tax time is hard upon us. Is there anyone here who does not have a gnawing fear of that notorious agency, the IRS, and its power? Are you aware of these facts?

• That the IRS can order a printout at any time of every bank transaction you have engaged in going back eight years? And they can do this without even notifying you. I suggest that you read the Fourth Amendment to the United States Constitution, which guarantees American citizens the right "to be secure in their persons, houses, papers, and effects against unreasonable searches and seizures."

• That all of the above-mentioned federal agencies can use drug-related RICO (Racketeering Influenced and Corrupt Organizations Act of 1970) and forfeiture laws to actually rob citizens of their property on even the alleged *suspicion* of drug trafficking or so-called "money laundering?"

• That the IRS has been accused (again, correctly) of using its power to intimidate citizens (through the threat of tax audits and other harassing tactics) who "cross" them or oppose the incumbent administration?[11]

Biological/Chemical Tests on Citizens

Now we come to a facet of federal government operations that I found difficult to believe, even after coming upon the information, but it is all documented.[12] Beginning in 1949 and continuing until the late 1960s the Department of Defense conducted a number of tests on American citizens *without* their knowledge or consent. Biological simulants *Serratia marcescens* and *Bacillus globigii*, and others, were used. Here is a sampling of sites where these involuntary tests were conducted:

1949-1950	Washington, DC	SM, BG
1950	San Francisco, CA	SM
1953	Panama City, FL	SM, BG
1955	State Highway, #16, PA	BG
	PA Turnpike (Tunnels:	
	Kittakinny & Tuscarora)	BG
1957-1958	East of Rocky Mountains	FP
1963-1964	Ft. Greeley area, AK	BG, FP
1965	Washington, DC National	
	Airport & Greyhound	
	Bus Terminal	BG
1965	Victoria, TX	LP, FP
1966	San Diego, CA, off California Coast	BG
1966	New York City subway	BG

> Note: BG = *Bacillus globigii*
> SM = *Serratia marcescens*
> FP = Florescent zinc cadmium sulfide
> LP = *Lycopodium Spores*

In the 1950 San Francisco test a navy ship released SM along the coast to determine how far the *Serratia marcescens biological* simulant would travel inland. The SM traveled 50 miles inland. In 1951 there were 11 cases of SM infection; one person died. The 1966 New York subway experiment was done by the CIA to determine if the subway system would be vulnerable to biological attack. In the 1955 Pennsylvania Turnpike tunnels experiments, *Bacillus globigii* biological simulants were sprayed into the air so it would be breathed by citizens driving through the tunnels. Hospital records were checked to see how far away the infectious biologicals were carried.

It is important to realize that these experiments in the public domain were done *without* either the *knowledge* or *consent* of the "subjects" being experimented upon. At first, the Congressional Report from which this information is derived indicates that the federal officials involved believed that the simulants used were rather harmless. But even after it was discovered that they were harmful, the experiments continued for 17 years before being terminated. Question: Are American citizens to be treated like guinea pigs at the will of their political "masters?" Question: Are similar tests *still* being conducted on unwilling citizens?

The military personnel testifying at the Senate Hearing came as close to admitting wrongdoing as we might expect under the circumstances. They assured the Senate Committee that such testing has been stopped. But something new has recently raised its ugly head: Retired Air Force Captain Joyce Riley, R.N., has been working with thousands of very sick Gulf War veterans who have—along with their wives, children, and the nurses and doctors who have been treating them—succumbed to the dreaded "Gulf War Syndrome." The Veteran's Administration has been telling these sick Gulf War veterans that their "alleged sickness" is only something they are imagining! Yet, the American Gulf War Veterans Association has documentation, dated September 9, 1993, that proves the federal government knew of chemical and biological exposure of US troops in the Gulf War.[13]

The important questions to ask are these: Have biological experiments indeed been going on in spite of the government's statements that they have stopped? Is this yet another indication of a tyrannical governmental system that has gotten out of control and which must be brought back under constitutional control?

Monetary Manipulation and International Monetary Collusion

The Federal Reserve System was foisted on the American public in 1913 under false colors after a secret "duck hunting" expedition on Jekyll Island, Georgia, in 1910. The secret meeting was sponsored by the Eastern money elite and Congressional leaders. The Federal Reserve System has faithfully served this money elite ever since.

Without the Federal Reserve, it is doubtful whether we would have gotten involved in World Wars I and II the way we did. Rather than protect the value of the U.S. dollar, Federal Reserve "protection" against inflation has steadily reduced the real value of the dollar downward. For instance, the purchasing value of the 1940 dollar, adjusted for inflation, is now less than seven cents!

Somehow, we must find a way to abolish this unconstitutional monster of monetary tyranny. It has the ability to insidiously inflate and deflate the money supply at will, and thus manipulate interest rates and the dollar value of capital wealth. This process works to the gain of those citizens whose wealth thereby increases, but it does so at the expense of other citizens whose wealth somehow seems to mysteriously melt away. And it is always the ordinary hard-working, monetarily unsophisticated American citizen who is shorn like a lamb in the process.

America has many hidden tyrannies that have been built into our politico/economic system, and the misnamed Federal Reserve System—with its close connections with the leaders of large international banks in our country and other countries— is one of the most hurtful. This in spite of the constant educational propaganda program that has built a false esteem of America's central-bank monster in the eyes of the unsuspecting American public.

The chief of Japan's central bank, capital markets division, is at this moment being prosecuted for accepting gifts in exchange for leaking information to the Industrial Bank of Japan and Sanwa Bank about the Bank of Japan's open-market operations. The Bank of Japan is to Japan what the Federal Reserve Bank is to our country. How much of this same type of advance leaking of planned open-market operations goes on in these United States of America is anyone's guess. Less than a year ago, a small news item hit the news about some suspected leaking of information from a source in the Federal Reserve

Bank, but further information was apparently effectively squelched because nothing more was heard of the matter.

Biblically, we know that man's heart is deceitful above all things and, therefore, cannot be trusted (Jer. 17:9). Yet, the American public has been conditioned to blindly trust the money manipulators in the Federal Reserve System who have the very same kind of "buddy-buddy" relationships with leading banks in this country that monetary officials in the Bank of Japan have with banks in their country.

Right now the American public has been strangely complacent about our country's lending of billions and billions of dollars, through the combined clandestine efforts of the Federal Reserve Bank, the International Monetary Fund, the World Bank, and the central banks of the "Asian meltdown countries."[14]

Question: Who are the primary beneficiaries of this international collusion in so-called "international monetary cooperation?" Answer: Mainly the large American banks that made risky loans to the so-called "Asian Tiger nations" which were growing so rapidly, largely as the result of the kind of international monetary collusion that the leaders of the Federal Reserve Bank and the leaders of those Asian nation's central banks have been engaging in for years. The result of the "international monetary cooperation" (which is just a sweet-sounding euphemism for what is more accurately called international monetary *collusion*) has been massive deficit spending in our country which has been thus "exported" to the Asian nations who now cry they need to be bailed out.

The "false-whiskers" story that was sold to the American public by the Federal Reserve and the big American banks, that otherwise stood to lose billions of dollars in loans gone bad, is that we had to come to the aid of the Asian nations to prevent a financial meltdown that would then hurt the average American. The same false story was spread through the news media to pave the way for our coming to Mexico's aid not long ago, and also to the financial aid of Brazil and other countries in South America before the Mexico meltdown.

In each and every instance the main beneficiaries have been the large banks with billions of dollars of risky international loans that were going sour. In each instance it was the American taxpayer—seduced by false propaganda generated by our government leaders, by the leaders of the Federal Reserve Bank, and by the large banks saddled with high-interest-rate loans that were going sour—who stood in the gap and unknowingly accepted the financial risks involved in the bailouts.

President Andrew Jackson excised the financial "monster" that was called the Second Bank of the United States in his day (1832). If Jackson were alive he would once again pick up the cudgel to perform the same good service to American citizens today! We should pray that the Lord will once again raise up political leaders like Jackson for us today. I love the study of money and banking, and I taught it for many years. But I hate and detest high-level money manipulation and financial perfidy!

Licensing Laws

There are special-interest coalitions between our state governments and the federal government. It has resulted in an oppressive tyranny that costs American taxpayers billions of dollars in extra expenditures every year as well as an important loss of freedom. I don't believe that the coalition that exists today was planned to be as it is, but rather that it has been the natural outworking of forces that were put in place long ago, and which have been naively accepted by the people. What am I referring to?

It is this: Many years ago special-interest groups in various occupations sought to increase their own incomes and public esteem by petitioning state legislatures to license the practitioners of their profession. (The process continues today.) I think of my father-in-law, a man of high integrity, whom I loved dearly before the Lord called him. He worked as an engineer. The State of Missouri passed a bill to license engineers and, as is often the case, the bill included a "grandfather clause" which would automatically license those persons who were already practicing in the profession. To his own financial detriment, but to my everlasting admiration, my father-in-law stood on principle and refused the bait of government-created higher income and increased esteem. He refused to be licensed by the state!

Now, the coalition of which I speak today is not the licensing of engineers, electricians, bricklayers, plumbers, or the many other licensed professions. The licensing of any profession by the civil authority is just as evil in practice as the profession I am about to zero in on. Let me state clearly that *any* government licensing of professions is contrary to God's law and an act of tyranny against the public.[15]

The one profession that has carried this ungodly practice to the greatest extreme is the medical profession, because it has combined the power wielded at the state level with the power wielded by the federal government.[16] In zeroing in on the medical profession, I do not mean to personally attack the integrity of the many fine persons who sincerely dedicate their lives to improving the health and physical well-being of sick people. Let me emphasize that I am focusing on the economically hurtful and freedom-robbing *system* that has evolved as a *result* of licensing. I am not focusing on individual practitioners, though they, of course, do indeed benefit personally from the system that has been put into place.

By 1900 most states had already licensed various professions. In 1910 the Carnegie Foundation commissioned Abraham Flexner, an historian whose brother was the medical dean at Johns Hopkins University, to investigate the medical schools that then existed in these United States of America. Flexner's recommendations resulted in the licensing of medical schools and thereby led to the demise of half of the existing schools of medicine. This drastically restricted the number of incoming medical students and thereby severely reduced the future number of medical practitioners. In 1928 the former head of the American Medical Association's Council on Medical Education stated that

> [T]he reduction of the number of medical schools from 160 to 80 (resulted in) a marked reduction in number of medical students and medical graduates.

We had anticipated this and felt that this was a desirable thing. . . . [17]

Certainly the leaders of the AMA would regard a reduction of practicing physicians as a desirable thing, because it would powerfully boost the incomes of the reduced number of practitioners who survived the legal purge. Question: Why not have the states license *every* line of work and *every* school that trains everybody? Then *everybody* can earn a higher income as a result of keeping out the so-called quacks! The answer is obvious: Such immoral systems cannot be extended to all workers because there must remain a large segment of the population to pay the tab. Since the incomes of all citizens cannot be raised by such schemes, the schemes have to be reserved to a relatively small elite. This explains why more and more professions today are following the lead of the medical and the legal professions. They want elitist status too! But eventually the system must either break down or end up with an unworkable medieval guild system that strangles in its own bureaucracy.

But the immoral system I am speaking about did not just stop with the licensing of medical doctors and of medical schools by various states as a result of the devious work of the AMA. During the "progressive era" of American history, Congress passed a bill which established the Food and Drug Administration (FDA). The FDA has grown into an enormous government bureaucracy that wields frightful power. The large food and drug companies the FDA was established to regulate now effectively run *it*. This has been a common happening in all government-regulated industries, and it can be roughly measured by the "musical chair" transfer of executives between the controlling agencies and the supposedly "controlled" companies. In actuality, the large companies in each industry *welcome* costly restrictions because such restrictions hurt small entrepreneurial companies more than the already-established large companies. The FDA also now has its own armed "swat teams" that make raids on medical practitioners who refuse to "toe the line" as well as on health food stores that sell "unapproved" safe-non-toxic herbs, natural foods, and non-prescription health supplements. All of this vicious government activity is done under the guise of eliminating the supposed "threat to health" generated by unlicensed practitioners as well as by licensed "maverick" practitioners. And the moving force behind this vicious activity is professional greed to enhance ones' own income and professional esteem in the community.

Are There Solutions?

I have spent some time in describing and discussing many problems of tyranny that exist in American society. I could go on and on, but we have looked at enough for one day. Now we ask, "Are there solutions to these problems?" The answer is yes, **BUT!**

While there are solutions, the ones I offer definitely *will not* be "politically correct" because they go against the mainstream of public opinion, and public opinion has been thoroughly manipulated and massaged by hidden forces and special interests for decades and decades. How many people do you know, for instance, who would readily agree with doing away with all licensing laws or the Federal Reserve System? Your answer shows the great need we have to remove the many "false whiskers" that now hide the truth behind the various issues I have raised. Every single solution I am about to suggest is truly workable *in theory*, but none is actually workable in practice in the absence of the *mental, spiritual,* and *moral* enlightenment that is needed to get each accepted and implemented. Thus, we are confronted with a challenging educational task.

First, and most basic, we must recognize that God is still in control and that all of the problems I have mentioned are indeed part of His developing plan in bringing about the establishment of His Kingdom on earth. This does not mean that we can "sit back and enjoy the ride," so to speak, and be content with the status quo, but rather that we should contemplate these problems in light of God's word and be much in prayer while seeking His guidance. God never said we would *not* be faced with challenges. God works through His people. Our job, as I see it, is first to conform our personal lives to the dictates of God's word and then to reform and reconstruct our society and all of its institutions according to biblical precepts. Every Bible-directed Christian is at heart a reconstructionist, in the sense that we as Christians are called upon to bring all of our social institutions into conformity with the mind of Christ (II Cor. 10:5).

Next, we should study each of these issues—as well as many issues I have not had time to touch upon—not only in conformity with God's word, but also in light of the Constitution of these United States of America. Generally I believe we will find that the two are harmonious, but, where they are not, we should work to conform our man-made document to be in harmony with God's spoken document, the Holy Bible. I realize that these are general statements, but they are necessary starting points for the work at hand. Our first and major challenge is to conform ourselves spiritually to God's heart and mind, to "bring into captivity every thought to the obedience of Christ" (II Cor. 10:5). Only then can we face the daunting task to reconstruct all of our societal institutions, including the institution of civil government.

Then, we need a widespread educational movement to help people relate God's word, the United States Constitution, and sound economic reasoning to the issues at hand. This calls for action on various fronts: We need the pastors and elders of our churches to speak out forthrightly in sermons and in Sunday School classes on the burning issues about which we are concerned so they can instruct their flocks about how God's word bears on the pertinent issues of our day. And, yes, this *will* mean that they must speak on issues that many church leaders wrongly perceive as "political" or as "politically incorrect." After all, who was it that was called the "Black Brigade" in the years leading up to and during the Revolutionary War? Why, it was the *pastors* of our churches who so faithfully instructed the people on biblical principles concerning governmental tyranny and other matters of state. It was common for pastors to instruct their congregations on important political issues in annual election-day sermons. If I might paraphrase Admiral Farragut in 1864 when he cried, "Damn the torpedoes! Full speed ahead!" Today's cry of Bible-believing, patriotic pastors should be, "NO government-bestowed tax-deduction! Let's tell it like it really is! Christ's church has *always* been **tax-exempt** because it is *outside* of the government's jurisdiction to levy taxes on it or to control it, therefore the Church has *no need* to seek tax deductibility!"[18]

Part of this widespread educational program should also include the formation of home-study groups for studying the Bible to become biblically oriented in our personal lives and public affairs, plus the formation of home-study groups to study our various State Constitutions and the Constitution of these United States of America.

Too many people, Christians and non-Christians alike, have little or no desire to apply God's word to God's institution of civil government or to the study of economic principles. Few people have even the vaguest understanding of the Constitution. Nor have they any perception at all when their elected representatives so often fail to uphold the oath that each elected official took—to uphold the Constitution and to protect it from enemies, both foreign and *domestic*. (Please note that very important last word.) For many years I would advise my students that I did not fear *foreign* enemies as much as I fear the civil rulers of our own country. It is because of these *domestic* enemies, who have failed to live true to their oath to uphold the Constitution—be it either the result of their ignorance of the Constitution, or of their intentional efforts to subvert its clear provisions—that we must be always on our guard if we are to preserve our liberty and self-responsibility before God.

Now to get down to specific recommendations for correcting the problems I mentioned:

✦ There is absolutely no constitutional basis that allows Presidents to rule by Executive Order. Laws can only come into being constitutionally through proper legislative process, which our founding fathers purposely made to be a *slow* and *laborious* process. Haste generates the rise of tyrants. This is exactly what happened during the Roosevelt Administration with the amending of the 1917 "Trading With the Enemy Act" in 1933 which produced the "War Powers Act."

Since 1933 Americans have been living with their precious God-given freedoms *unprotected* by the Constitution. This is just a statement of a cold, hard fact! Any incumbent president (and the existing holder of that office is offensively notorious for his pro-Marxist, anti-American demonstrations in Moscow and other European cities during his youth) can, at any time, for any reason he might conjure, declare a national emergency and thereby immediately impose totalitarian control over every aspect of your life and my life.

Dear liberty-loving friends, we are close to losing our Republic! The scary truth about this should *immediately* and forcefully be communicated to every citizen in our country. We *cannot* rely on the establishment news media to do so because they are part of the problem. The news media have *intentionally* covered up and failed to expose the slippery slope we, as a nation, are now sliding down. I challenge and encourage each of you to serve God and your fellow countrymen by sounding the cry of alarm. Be a watchman on the wall (Isa. 62:6). Our enemies are at the gate!

One practical step we can take regarding this issue, as well as others that I have yet to mention, is to apply the biblical principle of *governmental interposition*. This involves raising up intermediate magistrates and rallying behind them to oppose tyrannical rulers. I have covered this very workable principle in detail in a book entitled *Reclaiming the American Dream*,[19] so we will not go into how it works at this time. But be warned that time is short! We must act soon if we are to have any hope of restoring freedom in our country. If we do not act soon, I fear that armed resistance will be necessary, and no sane person wants that.

◆ The plan outlined in *State Department Document 7277* in 1961 is not on hold, it is *still* very much in effect. It is in the process of being implemented, sometimes quietly and other times audaciously. We must *very soon* rise up and demand that our military personnel be recalled immediately from the many "peace-keeping" (but, actually, warmongering) missions to which they have been assigned unconstitutionally in countries all over the world. These foreign assignments create hatred of America in foreign countries. We should heed President Washington's advice in his Farewell Address to engage in peaceable trade with all nations, but *not* to get involved in their wars and internal struggles. The world is an evil place to live because men are sinful. The civil government of every country has only one calling given to it by God, and that is to maintain law and order *domestically* and to protect its citizens from foreign aggressors so that they can live as self-responsible persons before God. This is the message we must communicate to our loved, but-still-asleep, fellow citizens of all races and of all creeds.

✦ There are treasonous forces in our country who are working covertly to undermine the Constitution of the United States of America. But, thankfully, because of the tenuous but still-existent bonds of the Constitution, and also because of the happy fact that many citizens still have firearms[20] with which to defend themselves, they are as yet hesitant to impose martial law at this time. To impose martial law, our political leaders must first create an imaginary "threat" or other excuse to declare a national emergency that will appeal to a majority of our unaware citizens.

We have valid reasons to suspect that the federal government was involved in the bombing of the National Trade Center in New York, the bombing of the Murrah building in Oklahoma City, and the crash of the airliner at Gander Mountain, Newfoundland. Each of these instances has been used to stir up a fear of terrorists among the public and, therefore, to create a supposed need for more federal gun controls and regulation of the population.

We know from the film taken with a FLIR (Forward-Looking Infrared) camera by a circling aircraft at Waco, Texas, that the federal agents there actually *murdered* women and children as they attempted to escape from the burning flames of the caldron in which they were confined. If you doubt what I am saying, please view the award-winning video which is currently being sold and distributed with the hope of awakening a sleeping populace.[21] I have seen this heart-wrenching video; it is enough to make a grown man weep for the victims of that tyrannical act of despotism and to weep for our Republic that once was! Every citizen in America should see this video!

✦ Another step patriotic Americans should insist on is the *immediate withdrawal* of these United States of America from the godless United Nations. As mentioned previously, one current plan to undermine our constitutionally protected rights is to ensnare us in UN-engineered treaties to ban U.S. citizens from owning guns and to force us to adhere to international laws concerning "environmental protection" that America must adhere to, but not other countries. This would entail the de-industrializing, and thus economically weakening, of America versus foreign countries. Thanks to our political leaders' practice of involving us in so-called "peace-keeping" activities all over the world, many of these countries now regard America as their enemy (Somalia, for instance).

✦ There are many government control agencies which now regulate practically every aspect of American life. (Have you flushed a 1.6 gallon toilet lately? I think of government controls every time I do so.) These control agencies constitute the practice of *fascism*, a form of socialistic government controls. This is the type of national-socialist regime which existed in Mussolini's Italy and Hitler's Nazi Germany. Yet, Americans have been brainwashed, not only, to accept, but to *embrace* such control agencies. Most such control agencies—and there are more than 80 of them in our country—have been imposed on us under the "Interstate Commerce Clause" of the Constitution. Practically every such agency is unconstitutional. Many are the result of Roosevelt's "Supreme Court packing" attack during the 1930s. We must work to disband them, but first comes the need to edify the saints and to instruct freedom-loving fellow citizens.

✦ The government biological tests I mentioned and documented are only part of the story. I did not mention the forty-year "Tuskegee Project"[22] involving 400 Alabama Negro men who had syphilis. The aim of that project was to study the progress of the disease without treatment. The study lasted from 1932-1972. Nor did I mention the experiments the federal government conducted by giving men in the military, *without* their knowledge or permission, hallucinatory drugs such as LSD to see how they reacted.

The French writer Frederic Bastiat, in his book entitled *The Law*, published in 1850, complained that the socialists of his day regarded citizens as nothing more than clay to be molded however the political leaders saw fit. Has our out-of-control federal government, with its many socialist/fascist agencies shown itself to be any different? This kind of information needs to be widely disseminated to awaken the public to the dangers of a government that has gotten out of control.

◆The Federal Reserve System was "sold" to the public under false colors. Senator Lindbergh, father of Charles Lindbergh who was first to fly across the Atlantic Ocean, and some other stalwart defenders of the Constitution opposed the Federal Reserve Act. But the high powers behind the Act (See Eph. 6:12) were too much for them, and a misled public embraced this financial monster, wrongly believing it was designed to give them economic stability through a "flexible" currency. Nothing could be further from the truth. Under the regime of the Federal Reserve, we have had the *planned demise of the gold standard*, which used to guarantee citizens the right to exchange their government-created dollars for real gold coins. Under its regime we have also lost the silver coins that used to jingle in my pocket as a boy. Under the regime of the Federal Reserve Bank the U.S. dollar now retains only a minuscule fraction of the purchasing power it had in 1913 when Woodrow Wilson signed the Federal Reserve bill into law.

With help from the Federal Reserve in financing government deficits, we got involved in World War I, World War II, the Korean War, the Vietnam War, and countless "peace-keeping" forays in foreign nations ever since. The Federal Reserve Act and the Income Tax Amendment (which I have recently discovered was never constitutionally ratified or passed into law) work hand-in-hand to pauperize the American people and to enslave them under the very officeholders who are supposed to be their civil servants.

✦ Somehow the federal government's open-ended power of taxation must be done away with, and the answer is *not* to impose a flat income tax or to change from an income tax to a national sales tax. The only *safe* answer to prevent a recurrence of the centralization of power we have witnessed all through the 20th century is to *return the taxing power back to the States!* This has been the great secret of Switzerland. The citizens of Switzerland hardly care who the head of their central government is, because he wields little power over them. But they *do* care who the political heads of their cantons (similar to our States) are because *that's* where the real taxing power resides. This was the way our federal government was originally supported under the Articles of Confederation, a system which that great Christian patriot, Patrick Henry, so ardently defended. His cry was, "I *love* those requisitions!" He feared a central government that could tax the people *directly!*

Any effort to restore American freedom will be fruitless unless the federal government's power to tax citizens directly is carefully emasculated. And then the Federal Reserve System should be replaced with a non-inflationary monetary system based on a gold-backed dollar combined with the restoration of silver dollars and subsidiary coins.

Next we should install, in place of the Federal Reserve Bank, for international finance purposes, a currency exchange board which would not attempt to manipulate currencies in order to peg the dollar to any pre-determined price. It is truly of no concern at all to the well-being of a country whether its currency rises or falls in the international exchange markets. Let free-market forces rule rather than politically-controlled monetary bureaucrats, who are always subject to being seduced and manipulated (Jer. 17:9). The international money market is the closest thing to a pure free market that exists. Economic production and the building of real wealth, because of the resulting existence of true economic freedom, would grow by leaps and bounds under such a free-market monetary regime. And so would true self-responsibility before God! Economic freedom, political freedom, and spiritual freedom are all closely entwined. The loss of one freedom threatens the continued existence of the other freedoms.

✦ Concerning licensing laws, little needs to be said. Pressures for government licensing of professions invariably comes from within the professions for the benefit of the professionals themselves. But the tactic used is always the evasive promise to "protect" the public. Do you remember the film, "The King and I?" When Anna suggested that the king call upon the British ruler for help against his enemies, the king replied, "No! I am afraid he will 'protect' me out of all that I own!" The Bible gives similar advice to those who would look to rulers for unbiblical protection, ". . . let me not eat of their dainties" is the advice given (Ps. 141:4; See also Prov. 23:1-3). The only godly "whole food" we should seek from our civil rulers is the biblically mandated principle of protecting our individual freedom and self-responsibility before God. Any other "dainty" received from the civil authority is sure to generate an unwholesome collusion between special interests and the civil authorities to share in stolen goods.

✦ Tax-supported education: One ubiquitous institution that needs to be eliminated, if there is to be any hope of rebuilding the spirit of freedom that once was characteristic of America, is tax-supported education. Early America, which astonished all of Europe with its rapid economic growth, was built upon a solid base of Christian education. Alexis de Tocqueville, in his book, *Democracy In America*, noted that the Bible was America's handbook.

The few early experiments in tax-supported education in America did not suffer from the many problems that are so evident in modern tax-supported education because the heart and soul of America from the 1600s through the late 1800s were still thoroughly Christian. But this beneficial Christian influence gradually began to wane as a result of the influence of Horace Mann, who was appointed Secretary of the Massachusetts Board of Education in 1837. Mann imported a statist Prussian form of education from Germany that was widely copied in these United States of America.

Since I have written about the inherent evils of tax-supported education elsewhere,[23] I won't go into detail here. Suffice it to say that tax-supported education is America's most widespread experiment in socialism, and we experiment on our most valuable resource, our own children! This is foolish! It is practically impossible through tax-supported education to foster the biblical ideals of one's ownership of self in subjugation to and in service to the ruling Lord of creation, of individual liberty, of political freedom, of private property, of the spirit of a voluntary society, and of the need for privacy from the civil authority. All of these ideals are sadly lacking among young people who graduate from the continuous indoctrination of a statist-oriented, tax-supported education. And the lack grows worse with each succeeding generation. Therefore, every tax-supported school in America must be disbanded and replaced with private and Christian-based schools or home schools in which parents are no longer inhibited from, but are encouraged to, exert their biblically-mandated duty of closely supervising their children's education.

Such a needed change from the suppressive influence of statist-oriented socialist education to the free atmosphere of private education will certainly not be easy, because Americans have long been seduced into accepting the seemingly "painless" expediency of educating their *own* children with *other* people's money through the State's power to levy taxes; but the change must be made if America is to survive as the "land of the free and home of the brave."

♦ Christian Jural Societies: Earlier I mentioned the War Powers Act of 1933 and how it has set the stage for the imminent imposition of martial law. This has also fatally affected the operation of our court system, which is now based more on *martial law* (i.e., arbitrary brute force) rather than on biblically based *common law* principles. Is there an answer to this problem short of the peaceful use of governmental interposition— or, failing that—the outright use of revolutionary force?

Again, the answer is yes. I believe the answer may possibly lie in establishing modern-day Christian Jural Societies based on the "Hundreds Courts" that once were used at the county level in medieval England. I am told that jural societies have existed for thousands of years.

Jural societies are being formed today, to reestablish Lawfully elected political bodies and provide their Christian members with a Lawful forum in which they can be self-governing Christians. It is the first line of defense to protect the life, liberty, and property of its members.[24]

I am in the early stages of investigating this medieval innovation of returning to biblically-based common law court procedure, so I cannot fully recommend it at this time, but the idea looks promising. I will welcome information and instruction from others who are more knowledgeable than I am.

♦ New Amendments to the Constitution: Is there a further solution? Yes, but it will not be a popular one to suggest, but here goes: We need a constitutional amendment that will prohibit the federal government from engaging in so-called "transfer payment" schemes. Also, we need an amendment that will prohibit any citizen from voting in an election at any level of government from which he or she receives a check (either as a wage, as a payment, or as a subsidy). It is exceedingly dangerous to allow citizens that have a financial interest in receiving money payments from a level of civil government to vote at that level of government. Why? Because recipients of government funds can be too easily "bought off" by the promises of political demagogues!

Today more than 30-percent of Americans receive one or more checks from the federal government every month. These include checks for all kinds of welfare payments, business and farm subsidies, and others. Most of these checks are equivalent to stolen goods in the form euphemistically called "transfer payment." They amount to nothing more than government-mandated *legalized theft*.

These programs of government-sponsored theft are endured by some and hungered after by others because an ignorant and unprincipled people have accepted the humanistic lie that a proper role of civil government is to take care of the poor and needy. But this is a duty that only falls on *individuals* and on *Christ's church*! It is an immoral experiment in breaking God's commandments against stealing and coveting for the civil authority to arrogate such unbiblical and unconstitutional power to itself. We, as Christian citizens, should get on our knees and ask God's forgiveness for taking part in such "legalized theft" programs and for allowing such an immoral travesty to happen. Then we should take immediate "politically incorrect" action to stop it.

In short, the objective of the suggested amendments is to disenfranchise those people who receive governmental largesse—whether they are employees of the government or in some way a recipient of funds from the government—from casting their vote at that particular level of government. I realize that such a radical idea (radical in a good sense) has no chance of "floating" at this time, but it surely would serve to restrict the massive voting influence of recipients of government "transfer payments." Such blocs of voting power can very easily overwhelm the votes of citizens who earn their incomes in the competitive marketplace, because the latter do not vote in blocs. Just think, even politicians and government bureaucrats would be restricted from voting for themselves! Can you think of anything better than that?

May our dear Lord bless, direct us and conform us to His word. May he grant us a winsome determination in reconstructing society and all of its institutions as we strive to build Christ's Kingdom until He returns.

Notes:

1 In short, any law, edict, or action by the civil authority, or by any other private or public entity, which breaks God's law or which runs contrary to our state or national constitutions amounts to an act of tyranny. Thus the saying about laws that extend governmental power beyond the limits of the Constitution: "an unconstitutional law is no law at all and has never been lawful from its conception."

2 Of course, this necessary constraint on human action—the absence of which would produce unrestrained license devoid of self-responsibility before God—is what creates the "rub" in human affairs. It is the proper balancing of man's freedom to act versus his need to be self-responsible before God that makes the formation of, and adherence to, a constitutional framework so very important to the happiness and weal of a nation.

3 John William, Randy Lee, and John Joseph, The Book of the Hundreds for edifying and preserving His church and state, Rev. 3.2, 2d ed. (n.p.:Christian Jural Society Press, 1996), 25.

4 House Bill #4960 which became law on October 6, 1917.

5 Congress, House, Trading with the Enemy Act, 65th Cong., 1st sess., H.R. 4960, Chap. 106 (6 October 1917), 411; quoted in Gene Schroder and others, War and Emergency Powers, (Campo, CO: American Agriculture Movement, n.d.), 60.

6 Henry Steele Commager, ed., Documents of American History, 7th ed. (New York: Appleton-Century-Crofts, 1963), 242.

7 Congress, House, National Banking System, 73d Cong., 1st sess., H.R. 1491, Chap. 1 (9 March 1933) 311; quoted in War and Emergency Powers, 59.

8 Brig. General Ben Partin, U.S. Air Force, Colonel James Ammerman, Ret. U.S. Army, and Lt. Colonel Joseph Arrigo, Ret. U.S. Army, "What's Happening to the United States of America," interview by George Douglas (7 February 1997), Blueprint for Survival.

9 Tom Rose, "The Many Faces of Tyranny and How to Establish Godly Rule (Part 1)," The Christian Statesman 141, No. 1 (January-February 1998): 28, n.8.

10 Monika Jensen-Stevenson and William Stevenson, Kiss The Boys Goodbye (n.p.: NAL-Dutton, 1991).

Jonathan Kwitny, The Crimes of Patriots: A True Tale of Dope, Dirty Money, and the CIA (New York: Norton & Co., 1987).

11 The IRS revoked a church's tax-exempt status because the pastor, Dan Little, addressed contemporary issues from a biblical viewpoint, in the case of Church at Pierce Creek v. IRS, U.S. District Court.

12 Congress, Senate, Subcommittee on Health and Scientific Research of the Committee on Human Resources, Biological Testing Involving Human Subjects by the Department of Defense, 1977, 95th Cong., 1st sess., 8 March 1977 and 23 May 1977.

13 For those of you that are interested in further information on the Gulf War Syndrome and Biological Testing, contact A.G.W.VA., 3506 Highway 6, South #117, Sugarland, TX 77478-4401 for copies of official government documents, books, videos, and audio cassettes. They are also available by calling (800) 201-7892, ext. 40.

14 The total amount of money that our political/financial leaders "coughed up" to rescue three of the "Asian Tiger nations," by monetary credit supplied at the ultimate risk of American taxpayers is stupendous. Here is a summary of the total credit supplied by the International Monetary Fund (IMF), the World Bank (WB), the Asian Development Bank (ADB), and other agencies who get a large portion of their funding from these United States of America: South Korea = $57 billion, Indonesia = $40 billion, Thailand = $17.2 billion; Total = $114.2 billion. International Monetary Fund quoted in: Fred Blahut, "You Bankroll 'Lender of Last Resort,'" The Spotlight, 23 March 1998, 21.

15 It is God who bestows spiritual and other gifts on men. See Exodus 31:1-6, I Corinthians 12:1-3, Ephesians 4:1. Since it is God who bestows the gifts, where do civil rulers get any legitimate right to license what God calls men to do?

16 Some people might argue that the licensing of the legal profession is even worse, and they may well be correct, especially when we consider the number of attorneys who end up in the legislative halls of our state and national governments as well as in our state and federal supreme courts!

17 Douglass C. North and Roger LeRoy Miller, The Economics of Public Issues, 5th ed. (New York: Harper & Row, 1980), 69.

18 For further information about tax-exemption see: Peter Kershaw, Hushmoney, (Branson, MO: Heal Our Land Ministries, 2000).

19 Tom Rose, Reclaiming the American Dream by Reconstructing the American Republic (Mercer, PA: American Enterprise Publications, 1996)

20 Recently President Clinton had a conversation with Prime Minister Tony Blair in which they discussed the disarming of citizens. Clinton said, "Give us time. You know, we have this thing called the Constitution."

21 "Waco, The Rules of Engagement." Available from International Business Systems, Inc., 1027 S. Pendleton Street, Suite #B-159, Easley, SC 29642; Phone: 1-864-294-1488 for credit card orders.

22 New York Times Index, 1995, 1242.

23 Tom Rose, "Tax-Supported Education," The Christian Statesman, Part I, September-October, 1995, 12; Part II, November-December, 1995, 28; Part III, March-April, 1996, 24.

24 William et al., The Book of the Hundreds for edifying and preserving His church and state, 44. Christian Jural Society materials are available through Randy Lee, General Delivery, Canoga Park Post Office, Canoga Park, CA. Phone (818) 347-7080; Fax (818) 313-8814.

INDEX

free, 16, 27, 31; self-interested nature, 30, 138, 145; self-responsibility to God, 12, 16, 18-19, 22, 28, 31, 82, 98, 102, 106, 141, 161, 166-167; tendency to plunder, 47-48, 53

Mann, Horace, 167

Marco Polo, 107

Martial law, 146, 149, 163, 168

Mental value imputations, 28, 52, 106, 171

Minimum wage laws, 54, 56-57

Monetary
inflation, 22, 35-36, 91-93, 95-99, 101, 113, 116, 119, 121-122, 129-131; manipulation/collusion, 115-116, 153; policy, 36, 114, 124-125

Money
laundering, 151; love of, 89

Monopoly power, 72, 140

Montreal Protocol, 73

Morgenthau, Henry, 117-118

Murrah Building, Oklahoma City, OK, 163

Mussolini, Benito, 34, 39n.15, 107, 140

Naessens, Gaston, 68-69

Neutrality about God, 12

Normative economics, 24-26, 34, 38n.2

North American Free Trade Assn. (NAFTA), 83

NAZI Germany, 34, 164

North, Douglass C., 64

Northwest Ordinance, 146

Parable of the talents, 106

Peters, Eric, 72

Political/social elite, 80

Positive economics, 24-26, 28, 38n.2

Power
arrogated by civil rulers, 33, 36, 55, 59, 146, 148; centralized, 29, 31, 34, 36, 136-137, 144; of the purse, 107

Presuppositions, 11, 23, 143

Price controls, 34, 54-55, 57

Process of voluntary persuasion, 52, 81

Proclamation of 1763, 71

Progressive era, 158

Propaganda
educational, 62, 66, 154; statist, 34, 44, 62, 66, 154, 156

Purchasing value of the dollar, 36, 101, 154

Quacks, 32, 59, 158

Racketeering Influenced and Corrupt Organizations Act (RICO) (1970), 151

Reconstruction Acts, 136

Reconstruction Finance Corporation (RFC), 118

Requisitions, 166

Rife, Royal Raymond, 67-68

Right to private property, 51

Roosevelt, Franklin D., 39n.15, 95, 101, 117-119, 122-123, 140, 146-148; administration, 93, 95, 124, 161; Supreme Court packing, 164

Roosevelt, Theodore, 112

Root, Elihu, 112

Sanwa Bank, 154

Schools
Christian, 168; home, 168; medical, 59-60, 63-66, 157-158; tax-supported, 136, 167-168

Scientific method, 24, 38n.1

Second Bank of the United States, 156

Smoot-Hawley Act (1929), 113

Social chaos, 82, 107

Social progress, 48, 51

Socialism, 22-24, 32, 39n.16, 44, 53, 59, 83-84, 96, 107, 114, 140, 164-165, 168

Special-interest groups, 57, 70, 73, 83, 85, 89, 94, 96, 140, 156

Specie reserves, 90, 107, 118, 121, 127-128

Sphere law, 28, 39n.11, 81

Spiritual freedom, 12, 15-16, 166

State worship, 53, 84

Stock Market Crash
(1929), 96, 115-117; (1987), 89, 96-97

Taxation, 36, 83-84, 94, 123, 139, 166

Theorem, 26, 38n.3

Theory, 73, 38n.4, 159

Third-party payment systems, 66

Thornwell, James H., 17, 18

Tocqueville, Alexis de, 167

Trading With the Enemy Act (1917), 146, 148, 161

Transfer payments, 18, 22, 34, 53-54, 140, 169-170

Treasonous forces, 163

Tuskegee Project, 164

Tyranny, 19, 29, 31, 39n.11, 39n.18, 139, 143, 145, 154, 156-157, 159-160

United States
Constitution, 29, 35, 37, 45, 73, 136, 139-140, 146, 151, 160-161, 163-165, 169, 172n.20; Export-Import Bank, 83; Publication 7277, 149-150, 162

Under-the-table payments, 78

United Nations, 31, 146, 149-150, 164; Biosphere Reserves, 150; collusion, 149; treaties, 150, 164; World Court, 150; World Heritage Sites, 150

Value, imputation of, 12, 25, 27-28, 30, 39n.10, 52, 103-105

SCRIPTURE INDEX

(Page references in parentheses)